CULTURE SMART!

NEW ZEALAND

THE ESSENTIAL GUIDE TO CUSTOMS & CULTURE

LYN MCNAMEE

D0710237

KUPERARD

"The real voyage of discovery consists not in seeking new landscapes, but in having new eyes."

Adapted from Marcel Proust, *Remembrance of Things Past*.

ISBN 978 1 78702 308 6

British Library Cataloguing in Publication Data
A CIP catalogue entry for this book is available
from the British Library

First published in Great Britain
by Kuperard, an imprint of Bravo Ltd
59 Hutton Grove, London N12 8DS
Tel: +44 (0) 20 8446 2440
www.culturesmart.co.uk
Inquiries: publicity@kuperard.co.uk

Design Bobby Birchall
Printed in Turkey

The Culture Smart! series is continuing to expand.
All Culture Smart! guides are available as e-books, and many
as audio books. For further information and latest titles visit
www.culturesmart.co.uk

LYN MCNAMEE is a New Zealand teacher and writer who has lived in and explored many of New Zealand's most beautiful locations. She currently lives on a sheep, grain, and hops farm in the mountains near Queenstown. After working with children for 30 years, Lyn turned to her second passion and began a new career as a writer. Having written a children's novel, she began blogging at lynmcnamee.com and writing articles for magazines, businesses, and Web sites at home and abroad. Lyn adores traveling, but having explored in the US, Europe, Singapore, and the UK, as well as New Zealand, she's discovered just how unique it is in the land that Kiwis call home.

CONTENTS

New Zealand, or Aotearoa (the "Land of the Long White Cloud"), as it is known by the Maori population, is a land of myth and reality, contrast and contradiction, rolling hills and glacial mountains, native bush and gentle farmland. Turquoise lakes, fast-flowing rivers, boiling mud, and leaping geysers add drama to the landscape, as do its unique flora and fauna.

New Zealand's culture is rich and diverse because of the numbers of people of different nationalities who have immigrated to the country. Britain's position as the main source country, which it held since early settlement in the nineteenth century, has been superseded variously in the intervening years by China, the Philippines, and India. New Zealand is also greatly influenced by its Maori heritage and today it is proudly recognized as part of its identity. Wherever you go, you'll see Maori art, traditions, place names, customs, and hear *Te Reo Maori*—the Maori language.

The New Zealanders are a friendly and welcoming people, who will go the extra mile to help you without expecting anything in return. As a nation of immigrants, they themselves have blended to form a unique persona, the Kiwi, who is used to newcomers and will be happy to accept you at face value. Kiwis are usually polite, gentle (off the playing field), trusting, and honest. They are also unpretentious, and are not impressed by airs and graces, preferring a more down-to-earth attitude. This comes from their roots in the early settler days, when men labored long and hard to "earn a crust," and luxuries were few. A memory of those early times remains, particularly in rural areas and among the older generation who did not have it so easy.

The renowned mountaineer, Sir Edmund Hillary—brave and pragmatic—has often been held up as an example of the spirit of New Zealand. He is quoted as saying: "In some ways I believe I epitomise the average New Zealander. I have modest abilities, I combine these with a good deal of determination, and I rather like to succeed."

"*Whanau*," or family, is influential in Kiwi culture. Many relatives live in the same towns and socialize as friends as well as family. When they have to move away, Kiwis will go to great lengths to travel home for holidays and special events. On the flip side, many immigrants left their families behind when they settled in New Zealand. These Kiwis congregate together, actively keeping their own cultures and customs alive while learning to live the New Zealand way of life.

New Zealanders love their land and the natural environment and passionately believe that everyone should be able to enjoy it. Aotearoa's moderate climate, relatively clean and green environment, reliable public services, and general safety make it an easy country to visit. *Culture Smart! New Zealand* explores the human dimension, offering tips and vital insights into Kiwi customs, values, and attitudes to help deepen your experience of this country and its fair-minded people.

Official Name	New Zealand	Member of the British Commonwealth
Capital City	Wellington	Metro pop. 417,000
Major Cities	Auckland, Christchurch, Hamilton, Dunedin	
Area	103,736 sq. miles (268, 675 sq. km.)	
Geography	New Zealand lies in the SW Pacific, SE of Australia. There are two main islands, the warmer North Island (NI) and the more rugged South Island (SI). The terrain is mainly mountainous.	NI has three active volcanoes, geysers, hot springs, Lake Taupo, and the Waipoua Forest. SI has the Southern Alps, the Canterbury Plains, and fiords in the southwest.
Climate	Temperate, with moderate to abundant rainfall	Summer Dec–Feb, Winter June–Aug
Currency	NZ Dollar	
Population	Approx. 4.9 million	Most people live on the North Island.
Ethnic Makeup	European 70.1%, Maori 16.5%, Asian 15.1%, Pacific Peoples 8.1%, other 2.2%	"Other" includes Middle Eastern, African, and Latin Americans.
Official Language	English and Maori. Maori is spoken by around 150,000 people, to varying degrees, and there is a conscious effort to keep it alive.	NZ citizens can request to be addressed in Maori in a court of law. Samoan is the next most common language, spoken by approx. 80,000 people.

Religion	Approx. 37% of the pop. is Christian, with Anglicans the largest group (15%), followed by Catholics (11%), Presbyterians (11%), and others. Nearly 50% claim no religious belief.	There are two indigenous Maori religions. Followers of Islam, Hinduism, and Buddhism number approx. 230,000 (around 5%) of the population. Judaism has been in the country since 1800s.
Government	Parliamentary democracy with a constitutional monarchy	Queen Elizabeth II, the Head of State, is represented in NZ by the Governor General. Seat of government is Wellington.
Media	Three major free-to-air TV channels; Sky Digital available to subscribers; many local TV stations as well as Maori TV. Over 200 radio stations	23 newspapers are published daily and over 50 locally published magazines.
Electricity	230 volts, 50 Hz	As Australia. 2 or 3 angle-pronged plugs are used. Adaptors are readily available for overseas appliances.
Internet Domain	.nz	
Telephone	Country code +64	
Time Difference	GMT + 12 hrs	Daylight saving from late September to early April, when time is GMT + 13 hrs.

CHAPTER ONE

LAND & PEOPLE

GEOGRAPHICAL SNAPSHOT

With the Pacific Ocean rolling onto its east coast and the Tasman sea pounding the west, New Zealand's long, narrow islands stretch from latitude 34° to 47° south, 994 miles (1,600 km) off Australia's southeast coast. New Zealand looks tiny on a map of the world, but at 103,738 square miles (268,680 square kilometers) it still takes days to drive from Cape Reinga in the north to the southernmost town of Bluff.

The country is home to around 5 million people, the majority of whom live in urban areas. Auckland, the largest city, has more than 1.6 million inhabitants while Wellington, New Zealand's capital, has around 415,000. Northland's Whangarei is currently New Zealand's smallest city, with a population of around just 40,268. While the cities teem with life, there are vast tracts of land across Aotearoa-New Zealand where you won't find a soul.

New Zealand's two biggest islands are simply named: the North Island and the South Island. In addition to

The towering hills of Mount Cook (Aoraki) and Mount Tasman (Horokoau) reflected in the waters of Lake Matheson, on the South Island.

these main islands are over 700 offshore islands, some with small populations. In the south, Stewart Island, or Rakiura, is perhaps the most well known—85 percent of the island is a national park. Great Barrier and Waiheke Islands are off the North Island coast while the Chatham Islands, 500 miles (850 kilometers) to the East, are the first in the world to see the sun each morning.

New Zealand may be small, but its landscapes are diverse. There are rolling green hills, dotted with sheep and extensive arable plains. Driving from top to bottom you'll pass dairy farms, pine plantations, vineyards, and orchards. There'll be stunning, sandy bays on the

east coast and craggy, rocky beaches on the west. On
your journey, you'll see more than seventy major rivers,
stunning lakes, and cross many winding mountain
passes. Dramatic snowcapped mountains and glaciers
backbone the South Island, while active volcanoes still
rumble in the North. In Taupo and Rotorua visitors
flock to the boiling mud pools, geysers, thermal
springs, and steaming mineral terraces.

Being in the Southern Hemisphere, northern parts
of the country are generally warmer than in the south,
with lush, subtropical forests and a long growing season.
Aotearoa is one of seven areas in the world where you

A sheep and her lambs on the rolling coastal hills of Christchurch.

can find temperate rainforests, most of them being on the South Island's West Coast. Much of the coastline is rocky, but there are also many bays, beaches, and harbors up and down the country where Kiwis and visitors love swimming, surfing, fishing, and sailing.

Volcanoes and Earthquakes

Sitting on the Pacific "rim of fire," New Zealand is often referred to as "the shaky isles." It was once part of the ancient Gondwana continent and is now on the boundary of the Pacific and Australian tectonic plates. These major plates steadily push and grind against each other, causing thousands of earthquakes each year, though you won't notice most of them.

Some are powerful and destructive. In February 2011 an earthquake destroyed parts of Christchurch, killing 185 people and causing billions of dollars' worth of damage. A further earthquake hit the Kaikoura coast, north of Christchurch, in 2016, closing the main Southern rail and road route for months. The New Zealand government has now made earthquake strengthening a priority for buildings, particularly in quake-prone areas, in order to minimize damage should another earthquake occur.

Most of New Zealand's volcanic activity in the last 1.6 million years has been in the Taupo Volcanic Zone extending from White Island in the Eastern Bay of Plenty to Ruapehu and Lake Taupo in the central North Island. The zone includes three frequently erupting cone volcanoes (Ruapehu, Tongariro/Ngauruhoe, and White Island) and two of the world's most productive calderas: Okataina and Taupo. Mount Ruapehu's 1996 eruption produced over seven million tons of ash, which affected visibility, disrupted air traffic, and ruined the winter ski season.

That eruption pales compared to White Island's 2019 disaster. Tourists had been visiting White Island for years to view the active volcano's abandoned sulfur works and desolate landscape. But in December 2019, the mountain top exploded, shooting a two-mile plume of rocks, ash, steam, and toxic fumes into the air. Boats and helicopters rushed to rescue the forty-seven tourists and guides on the island; sadly, twenty-two people died, and many others were severely burned. Unsurprisingly, the island is now off limits to all.

CLIMATE

"Long on mud and rain" is the perception of New Zealand's climate, and it's not altogether inaccurate. Auckland is estimated to have twice as much rain as London, but also twice as much sun! With seasons in reverse to most of the world, New Zealand's summer is a good time for northern hemisphere dwellers to visit, during their winter. February is usually considered the most stable month for warm weather.

New Zealand lies approximately halfway between Antarctica and the Tropics—"roaring forties" territory—and so it is prone to strong winds and stormy seas. Weather systems sweep in from the Tasman Sea, hit the Southern Alps and deposit rain onto the West Coast. The now-dry winds continue over the mountains, to parch the central and eastern regions. Consequently, West Coasters are well used to rain. Yearly rainfall at Milford Sound measures around 236 inches (600 centimeters). Franz Josef gets 157 inches (398 centimeters). In contrast, Canterbury on the east coast averages just 23.8 inches (60 centimeters) of annual rain.

New Zealand's climate is officially "cool to temperate," ranging from the sub-tropical north to inland snowstorms in both islands. There's a saying in Auckland: "If you don't like the weather, wait ten minutes." Another is "Four seasons in one day." Together these sum up how variable the weather can be in Aotearoa. There are four, discernible seasons:

- **Spring** September to November, unpredictable and variable.
- **Summer** December to February, mild in the south and warmer in the north.
- **Autumn** March to May, often extends to an Indian summer.
- **Winter** June to August, brings the rain in the north and snow in the south.

Temperatures rarely exceed 86°F (30°C) but fall below freezing in higher, inland areas and during southern winters. Happily, that also brings snow to the ski slopes. Winter averages around 57°F (14°C) in the north, and falls below 46°F (8°C) in Queenstown. Summer temperatures are between 70–75°F (21–24°C)

Milford Sound (Piopiotahi) is located deep in the Fiordland National Park on the West Coast and is part of the Te Wahipounamu UNESCO World Heritage Site.

in Auckland, and two or three degrees lower in Queenstown and Christchurch.

Most of New Zealand enjoys more than 2,000 hours of sunshine a year. Nelson and Blenheim in the south and Whakatane, the Bay of Plenty, and Napier in the north usually exceed 2,350 hours. Be careful when sunbathing: Auckland has the highest melanoma rate in the world thanks to breaks in the ozone layer over New Zealand. Summer weather forecasts include a burn factor, also known as the UV Index (UVI). A UVI below 3 is considered low, while a UVI greater than 10 is considered extreme. Schools teach the "Slip, slop, slap, and wrap" sun-safety message and insist on hats when playing outside. (**Slip** on a shirt, **Slop** on sunscreen, **Slap** on a hat, and **Wrap** on some sunglasses.)

Rich soil, mild temperatures, and plenty of sunshine make grape production possible even on the South Island, as seen here at Blenheim.

A MULTICULTURAL NATION

Humans only began migrating to Aotearoa around 1280–1350 CE, when Polynesians made the long, ocean voyage from the land the Maori called Hawaiki. Since then, immigrants from many nations have come to call New Zealand home. It is now very much a Pacific country, connected to the region by culture, history, politics, people, language, and shared interests.

Currently, around 70 percent of the population is of European descent—mainly English, Scottish, Irish, and Dutch—while 16.5 percent identify as Maori. Eight percent of New Zealanders are Pasifika (namely Samoans, Tongans, and Cook Island Maori). A further 15 percent are Asian, this number made up in large part by Chinese, Indians, Filipinos, South Korean, and Sri Lankans. The remainder of the population is classified as Middle Eastern, Latin American, and African (MELAA). Many New Zealanders nowadays identify with more than one ethnic group, and all are included in census statistics.

Maori are regarded as the indigenous people of Aotearoa and call themselves *Tangata Whenua*, which means "People of the Land," while those of European descent are sometimes called "*Pakeha*," a term that though originally meant something like "pale, imaginary beings" is not meant pejoratively.

By and large, the different peoples in New Zealand's melting pot live well together. However, Maori and the Pacific Islanders do not enjoy the same living standards as other groups, particularly those of European descent.

This, along with poorer health, lower life expectancy, and lower educational attainment, often leads to lower levels of income and greater unemployment. Inequality also affects many other groups: those with disabilities, women, single parents, senior citizens, the unemployed, and the undereducated. All this affects New Zealand's economic, educational, and social well-being, though there have been improvements in recent years. The recession and a rise in unemployment brought about by the Covid-19 pandemic have helped to highlight the systemic issues which are faced by around one-fifth of the population.

Problems for New Zealand's Maori began when the British began to colonize the country in the late 1800s and worsened as settlers and the Crown took control over increasing swaths of lands that had been home to Maori communities. Further issues arose when rural Maori transitioned to urban living, particularly after the Second World War. In 1951 only 20 percent of Maori lived in urban areas, but by 2001 they were as likely as the rest of the population to be living in cities or larger towns.

In 1971 the government appointed a race relations conciliator, now part of the national Human Rights Commission. The commission's job involves advocating and promoting respect, understanding, and appreciation of human rights across New Zealand society. It also provides information and a voice to those with issues that need to be heard.

Recent years have seen a resurgence of Maori identity. Many are becoming highly vocal about their loss of land and economic hardship, stating breaches of the 1840 Treaty of Waitangi. Te Tiriti, the treaty's Maori name, was signed by representatives of the English Crown and various Maori chiefs from the North Island. In it, the Maori ceded sovereignty to Britain in return for the rights and privileges of British subjects and the undisturbed possession of their lands.

In 1975 Parliament set up the Waitangi Tribunal as a permanent commission of inquiry to consider and award Maori land claims and treaty disputes dating back to the 1840s. Historical settlements with Maori *iwi* (nations, or tribes) aimed to resolve these claims and provide some compensation and redress. By 2021, seventy-three settlements had passed into law, with a further eleven awaiting confirmation at the time of writing. The Tribunal is still active today, investigating and making recommendations in ongoing land disputes.

Today, Aotearoa-New Zealand is very much aware of its bicultural heritage. There is a conscious movement to bring the Maori language, culture, and stories to the fore, and especially to reflect and promote these in schools throughout the country. There is also increased awareness that New Zealand is a multicultural society, including many nationalities and how these contribute to an identifiable, national lifestyle. The Asian population, two-thirds of which live in the Auckland area, has also had its share of problems and has been the target of anti-immigrant sentiment in the past. By and large, though, the many diverse groups that make up the multicultural fabric of modern New Zealand are welcomed by all.

A BRIEF HISTORY

The Early Days

New Zealand is short on human history—shorter than any other country in fact, as it was the last landmass in the world to be settled, though a precise date of settlement is still a matter of conjecture. Maori are considered to have been the first arrivals, coming from East Polynesia in the thirteenth century, the navigator Kupe being credited with discovering the country. However, the peace-loving Moriori tribe may have arrived at the same time or earlier, probably also from Polynesia, as they share similar ancestry with the Maoris, although their origins are more obscure.

Portrait of a Maori woman by New Zealand painter Gottfried Lindauer, circa 1890.

They made their home on the Chatham Islands, naming it Rēkohu, and formed a society that shunned aggression. It is believed that there were more than two thousand Moriori living on the Chatham Islands in the eighteenth century, but they faced total annihilation by invading Maori *iwi* from the mainland, who, taking advantage of the Moriois' pacifism, murdered and enslaved most of the island's population. Moriori numbers were further depleted by exposure to European diseases such as influenza. Today Moriori descendants live in the Chathams and abroad and are actively working to revive their culture and language.

Maori descendants trace their ancestry back to a fleet of canoes from Hawaiki, which is widely considered today to be Tahiti. As much of New Zealand's history dates from preliterate times, myth and legend have become intertwined with fact, so it is often difficult to separate the two, or to know when history takes over from, or replaces, tradition.

Maori legend says that the North Island was fished out of the sea by Maui, a demigod, hence the Maori name for the North Island is Te Ika a Maui ("The Fish of Maui"). Concerned that the gods might be angry about this, Maui went to make peace, leaving his brothers to argue about ownership of this new land. Their arguments turned to blows, and their pounding of the catch, or land, helped to create the mountains and valleys. Similarly, the South Island is known as Te Wai Pounamu ("The Waters of Greenstone"), and Stewart Island Te Punga a Maui ("Maui's Anchor").

The First Europeans

The first European sighting of New Zealand was in 1642 by the Dutch navigator Abel Tasman on his great "South Land" expedition undertaken to ascertain if "Terra Australis Incognita" actually existed. Explorers had searched in vain for this mythical southern continent for centuries before it was found, believing that it held many riches. It is thought that a Dutch cartographer gave New Zealand its present name because Australia was then called New Holland and so it was appropriate to name the new land after the other main province of the Netherlands, Zeeland.

It was the west coast of the South Island that Tasman saw and charted but, because the first encounter between Maori and Europeans off the coast resulted in the deaths of four Dutchmen, New Zealand was left to its "savage" inhabitants for more than a hundred years until James Cook arrived in 1769 on the first of his three voyages. Cook traveled around and charted both the North and the South Islands, and was amazingly accurate considering the navigation limitations of the time. He returned in 1773 and again in 1777, recounting in his journals his view that New Zealand was a land of promise, where settlers could build a comfortable life. Early European traders were more interested in making money than in settling, however. They turned substantial profits from whaling, sealing, and natural resources such as timber and flax.

A portrait of Abel Tasman circa 1637 by Dutch artist Jacob Gerritszoon Cuyp.

Dutch explorers during a skirmish with Maori at what is now called Golden Bay. Drawn by cartographer and artist Isaack Gilsemans who was aboard Tasman's expedition in 1642, it is thought to be the first European depiction of Maori people.

By 1839 both the Maori and British leaders were worried about the increasing lawlessness in Aotearoa. They were also concerned that the British colonial administrator Edward Gibbon Wakefield, through his business "The New Zealand Company," was buying vast tracts of land for paltry sums.

In 1840, Captain William Hobson was instructed to draw up a treaty between the Crown and the Maori. The treaty was then translated into the Maori language. This translation, called Te Tiriti, contained some crucial differences due to translation errors. In particular, the English version stated that Maori agreed to cede sovereignty to the Crown. However, in Te Tiriti, Maori were promised *tino rangatiratanga* (full chiefly authority) over their lands and resources. A signing ceremony was held at Waitangi, in the Bay of Islands, and copies of Te Tiriti were then taken throughout Aotearoa for other chiefs to sign. Both copies are known as The Treaty of Waitangi, which is now acknowledged and upheld as New Zealand's founding document.

War . . .

Relations between the Maori and Pakeha quickly soured. Maori became increasingly concerned about the effect the settlers were having on their society. At the same time, many Pakeha settlers wanted to start a new life on their own terms.

New Zealand's most renowned governor of the day was Sir George Grey. He was the principal author of the constitution of 1852, which granted white men but neither women nor Maori) the vote.

By 1854, the settlers had their own parliament, and two years later, a greater degree of autonomy. However, the situation between the Maori and the British continued to deteriorate due to disagreements over land, sovereignty, and Maori rights. It was a complicated time with battles fought particularly in Northland, Waikato, and Taranaki. The Maori called these wars Te Riri Pakeha ("the white man's anger"), while to the British they were known as the Maori Wars, and they continued until 1872.

. . . and Peace

In the 1870s, the colonists outnumbered the Maori for the first time when 100,000 (mostly British) immigrants arrived, including families with children. (It has always been a source of pride to Kiwis, and a point of differentiation from Australia, that their country was never a penal settlement.) New Zealand developed a small-farm economy with widescale sheep farming, and gradually became self-reliant. At the same time, the Maori were becoming increasingly marginalized. Settlers looked down on the Maori lifestyle and traditions and tried to assimilate them into British culture. During the following century, authorities banned the Maori language from being spoken in schools and as a result several generations grew up not knowing their language or seeing their culture valued.

In the 1880s the worldwide depression impacted on the country, resulting in low prices for wool, its main export. Although the discovery of gold in the South Island brought prosperity to this area, economic problems continued. Political parties emerged and the Liberal Party took office for the next twenty years (1891–1912), passing a series of laws to improve the quality of life. The government purchased large tracts of land to assist families to farm. Factory conditions improved, trade unions were encouraged, social security was implemented, and women's lives changed for the better. New Zealand prides itself on the fact that in 1893 it was the first country to grant women the right to vote.

By the turn of the century New Zealand had become

much more settled. A countrywide rail network was built, and on the communications side the telegraph, telephone, and penny postage were introduced. The workforce had become more organized, and professional groups such as doctors, teachers, and accountants formed national associations to protect their interests, as did employers, trade unions, and farmers. The land, no longer pioneer territory, had been largely tamed and cultivated. Sports, too, had become more organized, with the New Zealand Rugby Football Union established in 1892. New Zealanders had begun to develop a sense of nationhood and decided not to join the Australian federation of 1901. In 1907 New Zealand gained Dominion status within the British Empire.

The Emergence of a Nation

Ties with Britain remained strong and in 1899 New Zealand sent troops to South Africa to help in the Boer war, and did so again in the two World Wars. Thousands of New Zealanders died on various battlefronts, and the disastrous landing at Gallipoli in 1915 by the Anzacs, the joint Australian and New Zealand Army Corps, marked New Zealand's coming of age as a nation.

By 1886 more than half of New Zealand's European population of 578,500 had been born there, and people often identified themselves regionally as an "Aucklander" or a "Wellingtonian."

Settlers from different countries tended to congregate in different regions; for example, Christchurch was more English, Dunedin more Scottish, and Auckland more like

Australia. Thanks to the gold rushes of the 1870s the South Island's population remained larger until 1896. Most Maori lived in the temperate North, and this was where Maori and Pakeha fought for control of the land.

At this time, New Zealand's standard of living compared well to the rest of the world—social welfare measures were put in place, including widows' pensions, and maternity hospitals were built.

After a few prosperous years following the First World War, the 1920s were a time of hardship in the country, and the worldwide Great Depression severely impacted on New Zealand. Export prices for primary produce fell and the consequences were felt throughout the country. Unemployment in the towns and general discontent led to riots. A conservative coalition government failed to remedy the situation and a new Labour Party under Micky Savage, which took power in 1935, managed to revive an already recovering economy with solutions that concentrated on improving conditions for the average family. It extended the welfare state with the Social Security Act of 1938, began a state housing program, increased public works spending, and set up a health care system.

With the fall of Singapore to the Japanese in Second World War, New Zealanders realized that Britain could no longer be relied upon to guarantee their security and the country eventually proclaimed independence in 1947.

As the US had protected both Australia and New Zealand from Japan during the Second World War, New Zealand felt obliged to support it. In the 1950s it sent

GALLIPOLI

The Gallipoli Campaign was one of the great disasters of the First World War. The Allied strategy, brainchild of Winston Churchill, was to end the war early, creating a new war front by forcing a way through the Dardanelles and linking up with Russia. Turkey was allied to Germany, and the heavily fortified Gallipoli peninsula dominated the Dardanelles, the straits connecting the Mediterranean to the Black Sea. After failing to take out the Turkish batteries by bombardment from the sea, it was decided to launch full-scale landings. A combined force of Anzacs, the British 29th Division, and French colonial troops landed on the Turkish peninsula on April 25, 1915. The coast was precipitous, with few good landing places, and the combination of superior Turkish firepower and poor Allied generalship resulted in a bloody withdrawal in which 2,700 New Zealanders died and another 4,700 were wounded. The date has been kept as a day of national mourning in both New Zealand and Australia.

armed forces to Korea, to help the Americans in their fight against Communism. However, when troops were sent to support America in Vietnam, for the first time the New Zealand public voiced its opposition. There were fears that the conflict could escalate into a major nuclear war, and also the feeling that the Vietnamese should decide their own form of government. Later, this anti-nuclear stance brought New Zealand into conflict with the US and France who were conducting nuclear tests in the Pacific. New Zealand's protests led to French Secret Service agents planting a bomb on the Greenpeace ship Rainbow Warrior, which exploded in Auckland's harbor on July 10, 1985.

Postwar

The 1950s saw growing prosperity in New Zealand. The economy stabilized and many new industries such as the steel industry opened, and the country became more industrialized. Changes were made to laws to ensure equal opportunity for everyone, from job accessibility to housing and education, whatever the person's sex, race, ethnic origin, marital status, or religious beliefs. During this time, many more groups emigrated from Britain, Europe, and the Pacific Islands—Fiji, Tonga, the Cook Islands, and Western Samoa.

While New Zealand was affected by the 1970s oil crisis and the 1980s global recession, the most profound economic and psychological effect came when Britain joined the European Economic Community in 1973. The apron strings were finally cut! In 1986, the Constitution Act ended Britain's residual legislative powers, and New Zealand became solely responsible for its own government (which it had been, in effect, for years). It remains, however, a key member of the British Commonwealth.

Modern Times

Today, New Zealand is much more integrated into the world and, having shaken off its British past, is probably more influenced by America—it is no longer a colonial outpost of Britain but a multicultural Pacific nation. Nevertheless, Kiwis have not yet expressed a genuine desire to cast aside the monarchy and become a republic.

Aotearoa still opposes the testing and use of nuclear weapons and in 1984, Prime Minister David Lange banned nuclear-powered or armed vessels from entering New Zealand waters, and the country takes a prominent part in UN peacekeeping activities throughout the world. It has close relations with Australia at all levels of government, the respective prime ministers and cabinet ministers holding annual formal talks on issues such as health, education, and quarantine, among many others. The two countries cooperate closely internationally and regionally, specifically in the Pacific Islands Forum, and are currently involved in the Cairns Group, a coalition of seventeen agricultural exporting countries, which are seeking freedom of trade in agriculture. A treaty signed in 2004 by both countries defined maritime boundaries in the Tasman Sea and areas of the southwestern Pacific Ocean.

New Zealand shared a security alliance with Australia and the US (ANZUS) from the end of the Second World War until the mid-1980s. With Australia it established the Closer Defence Relations (CDR), which, although not a formal treaty, brings together many agreements on policy, intelligence and security, logistics, and science and technology. There has been significant operational collaboration between the two defense forces, including in Timor Leste, Bougainville, Solomon Islands, and Tonga. Forces from both countries amalgamated in operations in East Timor during the humanitarian crisis of 1999–2002 and in the Solomon Islands during the civil unrest and subsequent coup of 2000, forming a South Pacific security force.

In 2019, terrorism raised its ugly head in New Zealand when a gunman opened fire on people at two Christchurch mosques, killing fifty-one and wounding forty more. As a nation, New Zealanders were shocked and outraged at this attack, and thousands joined Muslim leaders and Prime Minister Jacinda Ardern in the mourning that followed. The attack triggered strict new gun legislation changes in New Zealand.

Covid-19

In 2020, New Zealand reacted swiftly to the news that a newly identified virus was spreading throughout the world. The government quickly introduced self-isolation rules and border closures to those from infected countries. By mid-March, Covid-19 was in New Zealand, and the country went into total lockdown. The coalition government introduced wage subsidies and several rescue packages to shield the economy from the worst effects.

By June, there were no active cases in the country, and, in contrast to much of the world, Kiwis could once again assemble freely. People were intensely proud of their collective response to the pandemic and the subsequent return to normal activities. Despite the relative success, the economic effects were far-reaching: businesses closed and others retrenched. Many Kiwis lost their jobs as a result of the restrictions, or worked on reduced hours, resulting in hardship for their families.

In 2021, New Zealand's border remained mostly closed to visitors. Without exception, all arrivals were required to isolate in managed facilities for at least fourteen days before joining the community. Sporadic outbreaks were quickly dealt with through brief but strictly enforced lockdowns and an ongoing vaccination program.

THE ECONOMY

New Zealand is a resourceful nation, largely due to its many and diverse immigrants, who arrived with little and had to look to the land to sustain them. The perception that it is a country of sheep and dairy farmers, where sheep outnumber the people, is not wholly inaccurate, but this does not reflect the present reality. For one thing, although there are indeed still more sheep than people, numbers are dwindling—there being today six sheep for every New Zealander where previously there were twenty. Farming is still the backbone of the economy, but traditional earners, which formed 90 percent of exports in the 1960s, have been joined by newer industries such as tourism, manufacturing, seafood, wine production, and filmmaking.

When Britain entered the EEC in 1973, 91 percent of New Zealand's butter and 65 percent of its meat (mostly lamb) were exported directly to the UK. But when Britain terminated the bilateral agreements farmers had to find new markets and products. The kiwifruit was one of these, as was the New Zealand-bred Corriedale sheep, which provides high-quality wool and meat. It has become the second-most important breed globally, after the Merino. Today, New Zealand's largest export market is China, followed by Australia, the US, Japan, and Korea, with the UK only in sixth place. According to the Organization for Economic Cooperation and Development, New Zealand is currently among the world's more prosperous economies.

Challenges: From "Rogernomics" to Climate Change

Kiwi farmers are some of the most skilled and efficient in the world today; they operate without subsidies in a competitive market, and face both high internal and external transport costs. Their market position and relative strength was not easily won. Much of it can be attributed to Roger Douglas, Labour's finance minister in the 1980s. In 1984 he decided that farming should not be treated as a revered institution, resting on its laurels and entitled to state protection, but should become a business like any other. Douglas instituted a program of deregulation, privatization, and downsizing. With the elimination of subsidies farmers became more focused on marketing. He reduced tariffs, removed quotas, lifted controls on prices, wages, and foreign exchange, and deregulated the labor market. As a tribute to its instigator, this free-market approach, the likes of which had not been seen before in the modern, Western world, was labeled "Rogernomics." It was seen as being so beneficial that, when Labour was voted out of office in 1991, Douglas's counterpart in the National Party, Ruth Richardson, continued the policy.

Among the most pressing challenges that New Zealand's economy faces are those posed by climate change, what Prime Minister Jacinda Ardern has called "the greatest challenge of our time." Having declared a climate emergency, the government set up the Climate Change Commission tasked with ensuring New Zealand becomes entirely carbon neutral by 2050—a goal enshrined in law. While everyone agrees it is an aim worth striving for, few are certain as to how to get there without causing considerable damage to the economy. For one, agriculture, manufacturing, and oil industries, among others, will all face increasingly severe penalties under the proposed plans, which some say could put them in jeopardy.

In addition, there are the economic challenges posed by the Covid-19 pandemic. In 2020, borders closed to international visitors and the country's otherwise prosperous and productive tourism industry all but withered overnight. New Zealanders themselves are keen travelers and so the domestic holiday market experienced an increase, but it could not make up for the lack of foreign tourists. The long-term effects of the pandemic on the economy remain to be seen, but it is expected that the tourism industry will return to strength once the global situation has been brought under control.

One plus side, in the short term at least, is that tens of thousands of Kiwis have returned home to New Zealand. Seeking the shelter of their homeland, they brought with them the skills and experience that they acquired abroad and as a result the local economy has benefited from something of a "brain gain." Time will tell how many settle back in Aotearoa for the long term.

Resources, Products, and the Environment

New Zealand has many natural resources: gold, silver, and coal are mined in various regions while iron is mined at Waikato for the country's steel mills. Oil exploration and drilling were in the past an important sector and export earner; however, in light of the government's decision to reduce New Zealand's carbon footprint, it was recently announced that there would be no further offshore oil and gas exploration permits granted. Instead, the country is pivoting towards securing greener and renewable alternatives. In 2021, 84 percent of the country's electricity was sourced from renewable sources including hydropower, wind, and solar. These, plus natural gas, account for 40 percent of Aotearoa's total energy needs—a figure that is set to increase in the coming years. The government has set a target of sourcing 100 percent of its electricity from renewable sources by 2035.

Tree planting has also received government support in recent years, especially varieties such as Radiate Pine, New Zealand's dominant species. In addition to providing tens of thousands of jobs in the forestry industry, trees provide a carbon sink and a place for Kiwis to explore and enjoy nature. Today wood constitutes New Zealand's third largest export after dairy and meat and contributes around 1.6 percent of the country's total GDP.

Seafood is New Zealand's eighth-largest export, with abundant salmon, white fish, oysters, rock lobster, tuna, and mussels available. Kiwis love the water—an estimated one in eight owns a boat—and the country is a leader in the marine and boat design industry. Thanks to its success in recent America's Cup regattas there is plenty of innovation in designing, building, and crewing racing yachts of all types.

New Zealand also has a thriving local movie industry. Unique and otherworldly scenery, accessibility, facilities, and expert Kiwi film crews mean that many blockbuster movies have been made in New Zealand in recent decades, among them the *Lord of the Rings* trilogy, *The Hobbit*, and *Narnia*, among others.

GOVERNMENT AND POLITICS

New Zealand is a parliamentary democracy in the Westminster tradition, with a constitutional monarchy. On her accession in 1952, Queen Elizabeth II was proclaimed "Queen of this realm and all her other realms," and she reigns over New Zealand independently of her position as Queen of the United Kingdom.

New Zealand's Governor General summons or dissolves parliament and acts as the Queen's representative. Chosen from New Zealand's citizens and appointed by the Queen on the prime minister's recommendation, the role is symbolic and ceremonial.

There is no upper house of parliament; the prime minister is the head of government and must have the House of Representatives' confidence to govern. The House is made up of 120 elected members who propose and pass the laws of the land and approve the raising and spending of money by the government. However, all bills need the Governor General's assent to become law. A government's term of office is three years, and while it is compulsory to register to vote, voting itself is voluntary. Since 1865, the seat of government has been in Wellington. Before that, it was in Auckland and prior to 1840 was in the Bay of Islands.

Interestingly, New Zealand does not have a written constitution or Bill of Rights. Acts of parliament direct how the country is governed, and certain customary rules are upheld. More acts of parliament safeguard specific rights. These include the Bill of Rights Act of 1990, which specifies citizens' rights when dealing with the government, and the Human Rights Act of 1993, which prohibits discrimination on various grounds.

The Voting System

All citizens and permanent residents of New Zealand over the age of eighteen years are eligible to vote, but only New Zealand citizens are entitled to sit in parliament.

At first, Aotearoa used a First Past the Post electoral system, whereby voters had one electorate vote and the party who won the most electorates formed the government. This sometimes led to a party winning the popular vote but still losing the election and as a result, in 1993 New Zealand replaced FPP with MMP, a Mixed Member Proportional system modeled on Germany's system. Here, each party draws up a list of parliamentary candidates in order of priority, and voters cast two ballots, one for their electorate and one for their preferred political party. In the seventy-two electorates, the candidate with the most votes wins the seat. However, the party vote decides the overall number of seats each political party gets, and so additional MPs are added to the party lists to ensure that each party can fill the correct number of seats proportional to their party's success.

By and large, MMP gives minor parties more opportunities to enter parliament and, as a result, coalition governments have become the norm. The issue is a subject of discussion among New Zealanders, who sometimes feel that a party will put more effort into accommodating its coalition partner over issues upon which they may differ just to stay in power, rather than finding solutions to problems that need addressing. Critics of the system also point out that disproportionate power is often given to minor parties whose support is required to form a government, and so are able to dictate terms well beyond what their mandate would otherwise justify. Still, parliament is now more representative of and responsive to the varied groups in Aotearoa. In particular, a Maori electoral roll represents seven Maori electorates throughout the country, and people of Maori descent may choose to be on either the general roll or the Maori roll.

The Legal System

While parliament enacts the country's laws, it is the judiciary that interprets and enforces them. Judges are appointed by the Attorney General and are expected to be apolitical in their rulings. They rule in District Courts, the High Court, the Court of Appeal, and the Supreme Court, which is the final court of appeal in the land. Courts operate on the trial-by-jury system, inherited from the UK, while judges act as neutral referees to the defense and prosecution. There are also special courts such as the Family Court and the Youth Court, both of which operate under the district courts sector; the Employment Court, which hears cases relating to the Employment Relations Act; and the Environment Court, which hears matters relating to the Resource Management Act.

In 1865, the Native Land Court of New Zealand was set up to facilitate the purchase of Maori land by the British Crown by converting traditional communal Maori ownership titles into titles that were recognizable under English law. In the 1950s it became recognized that the court's activities had had a negative effect on the Maori community, for whom land had previously been "*taonga tuku iho*," a treasure to be handed down. As a result, in 1954 the court's name was changed to the Maori Land Court, and steps were taken by the court to prevent further alienation of Maori communities from their traditional lands. Today, among its roles, the Maori Land Court serves to promote the retention, development, and use of Maori land by indigenous communities.

Political Parties

For many years, the dominant political parties in New Zealand have been the National (center-right) and Labour (center-left) parties. Since 1935, the National Party has formed five governments and the Labour Party six. Although elections are held every three years, a governing party may win consecutive elections and govern for several terms. Indeed, it is rare for a party to govern for only one term.

Many other parties have come and gone over the years, though few were able to secure seats in parliament under FPP. Since the change to MMP, however, smaller parties have had a much greater showing; New Zealand First, the Green Party, the Maori Party, Act, United Future, and the Alliance have all won seats since 1993. Some have formed part of coalition governments, while others have remained in opposition.

In 2020, the Labour Party made history by winning the election outright, the first party to do so since MMP was introduced. The landslide win was a vote of confidence for Prime Minister Jacinda Ardern and her calm, communicative leadership style during the Covid-19 pandemic. Ms. Ardern had previously headed a coalition government with New Zealand First and the Green Party in 2017–2020. In 2020–2023, although the

Labour Party ruled by a majority of 65 seats, it continued to work with the Green Party under a cooperation agreement, whereby the two Green Party co-leaders held portfolios outside the cabinet.

MAJOR CITIES AND AREAS OF INTEREST

The North Island

Te Ika a Maui is a land of lush forest and rugged bush, cosmopolitan cities, harbors, beaches, and offshore islands. From flat plains and rolling hill country to volcanoes and bush-covered mountain ranges, there is something for everyone here.

Auckland—the "City of Sails"—is home to one-third of New Zealand's population and covers a large urban area bordered by the Manukau and Waitemata Harbours. The city is built over 53 inactive volcanoes which provide breathtaking views, as does the iconic Sky Tower. Auckland has hosted the America's Cup yacht race three times. It has a vibrant, bustling wharf-side restaurant and café scene at the Viaduct, Wynyard Quarter, and Princes Wharf.

Northland and the Bay of Islands are steeped in history. The treaty of Waitangi was signed here, and the Maori explorer Kupe landed at the Hokianga Harbour more than one thousand years ago. Cape Reinga, where the Tasman Sea meets the Pacific Ocean, is a spiritual place for Maori and the northernmost point of the island. The Bays are famous for their big

Auckland's city skyline.

game fishing and many boating trips out around the islands. There's much to see in Northland, from Tane Mahuta, the giant kauri tree of Waipoua Forest, to the fabulous Hundertwasser buildings in Kawakawa and Whangarei.

Don't miss Rotorua as you travel south. With erupting geysers, bubbling mud pools, and the smell of sulfur permeating the air, the thermal areas hark back to the dinosaur age. New Zealand's capital city, Wellington, lies at the southern end of Te Ika a Maui and is home to approximately 550,000 people. Known, with good reason, as "the Windy City," it's a vibrant place full of quality bars, cafés, and restaurants and is home to the country's main seats of government: Parliament House and the Beehive.

Parliament House and the Beehive in Wellington, New Zealand's capital.

The South Island

Visitors to Te Wai Pounamu often feel as if they've entered a different country. Fewer people live in the "Mainland" (as it's often called), but they are fiercely proud of their island.

At the northern point, in sunny Nelson, you'll find stunning beaches, more bush-clad hills, and three of Aotearoa's thirteen national parks.

The West Coast is wild, wet, and rocky, with black, iron sand beaches. You'll find working mines and towns like Hokitika with its Shanty Town village, which gives visitors a peek into the past. Driving south, you can visit two spectacular glaciers, Franz Josef and Fox, although both are receding as the climate warms.

The Fiordland National Park is famous for the incredible beauty of its lakes and mountains. Visitors taking a boat trip out onto the pristine Milford or Doubtful Sounds are stunned by the sheer cliffs and 1000 ft waterfalls. Fiordland, along with Tititea (Mt Aspiring), Aoraki (Mt Cook), and the Westland National Parks, make up the UNESCO World Heritage Site Te Wahipounamu.

Queenstown, the South Island's premier resort, offers five ski fields in winter and adventure activities in the summer months. The city of Dunedin is known for its Scottish heritage and is the coldest of New Zealand's main centers.

Stewart Island, roughly 19 miles (30 km) south of the South Island, is great for bird lovers. It is home to the southern brown kiwi (*tokoeka*), blue penguin, and the rare, yellow-eyed penguin. With 174 miles (280 km) of

Mount Aspiring National Park.

walking tracks, the island is a hiker's paradise. Visit in summer but be prepared for rain at any time of the year.

New Zealand is a paradise for hikers, or trampers as they're known locally. Walking tracks vary from the bush and mountains of the Kepler Track near Te Anau to the volcanic plateaus and lakes of the Tongariro Crossing. You can even walk the length of Aotearoa on Te Araroa, The Long Path, which at a pace of 15 miles (25 km) per day takes about 120 days to walk. Cyclists are well served, too, with twenty-two "Great Rides" and many smaller trails spread throughout the country. See Chapter 7 for more on travel and how to get around.

Hikers enjoy the view at Tongariro Alpine Crossing.

CHAPTER TWO

VALUES & ATTITUDES

PROUD TO BE KIWI

New Zealanders today come from an assortment of nationalities and backgrounds, including Maori, Polynesian, British, Dutch, South African, Chinese, Indian, and Latin American. Over time they gained a sense of common identity, which has grown into the "Kiwi" persona.

On its journey to nationhood, New Zealand chose not to join the Federation of Australia, which was established in 1901, and become its seventh state. In 1948 a separate citizenship was created and the practice of calling Britain "home" more or less died out in the 1950s. Britain's national anthem, in use since 1840, has now been ousted by "God Defend New Zealand," with Maori verses sung before the English, and in 1977 was given equal status with the British anthem. In 1977 the words "British subject" were removed from the New Zealand passport.

Two national holidays every year have a distinctly nationalistic tone—Waitangi Day on February 6, which celebrates the signing of the Treaty, was declared a holiday in 1974, and Anzac Day on April 25, which commemorates the landing of New Zealand and Australian troops at Gallipoli in the First World War. New Zealanders will be impressed if visitors are aware of these two events.

There is no official national flower, but the silver fern appears on all national sports clothing and army insignia, and has become an unofficial emblem. The red *pohutukawa* and yellow *kowhai* flowers are also symbolic of New Zealand's summer and spring respectively.

The national flag being lowered on Anzac Day, held in April.

The New Zealand flag, which was based on the British Blue Ensign design of 1869, was adopted in 1902 but was officially declared the national flag as late as 1981. The four five-pointed red stars represent the southern constellation, although some consider that they were intended to signify the four countries of the United Kingdom. Australia, in contrast, has white stars loosely scattered on its flag, and it is a good idea not to confuse the two!

There had been numerous calls to replace the flag with a design more representative of the New Zealand nation. The debate, which had been going on since the 1970s, was finally settled at the Second Flag referendum held in March 2016. The process was a long and costly one. The Flag Consideration Panel judged 10,292 flag designs and shortlisted forty designs, which was whittled down to five alternatives that were put forward to be ranked in the first referendum, held in 2015. The Silver Fern Flag, designed by Kyle Lockwood, was chosen to stand against the old British Blue Ensign design. With the question "Which flag do you think best represents the shared values and beliefs and how we see ourselves now and into the future?" New Zealanders chose to stick with the status quo. (See page 84 for more on national colors and symbols.)

This keenness to be a Kiwi is part and parcel of an enthusiastic patriotism, which emphasizes the fact, and maybe acts as a reminder, that they are one nation, albeit a relatively new one. This may account for the Kiwis sometimes going "over the top," as in giving their winning America's Cup team of 2000 a ticker-tape parade down Auckland's Queen Street and only a year later castigating one of that team, Russell Coutts, for his decision to leave Team NZ and join a Swiss team because it was a more lucrative prospect. He won the America's Cup for Switzerland in 1993 and was, sadly, branded a traitor in certain circles.

You will go a long way with New Zealanders if you start by complimenting them on their country, and that is not hard to do, as it is a place of great natural beauty and charm. It is not uncommon to see various towns displaying signs saying, "Home of the world's biggest brown trout," " . . . largest fish and chip shop," or " . . . best ice cream." New Zealanders are also proud of their "hokey-pokey" ice cream, a sort of butterscotch offering, which they consider their unique invention. Shops and businesses also get in on the act and take it a step further by using the prefix "Kiwi," whether to describe food, sports, or more technical activities. Further, if "nz" can somehow be incorporated into a word then it must be done. New Zealanders, therefore, are EnZers, and many businesses demonstrate their patriotism by adapting their spellings accordingly. Companies are called Fernz, Newztel, Kidz First, and Kay-Zed Cruises, and there is even Split Enz, a rock group.

By and large, Aotearoa is an extremely safe country, and this is a point of pride for many Kiwis. Despite the shocking Mosque attack by a lone gunman in 2019, New Zealand ranked second on the 2020 Global Peace Index. The GPI measures the level of violence within a country and its contributions to international peacekeeping missions. On the whole, New Zealand's society is transparent, and rule-abiding; in 2020 it ranked as the least corrupt country in the world on the Corruption Perception Index, no small feat.

New Zealanders are also proud of their heroes, especially those who shine on the world stage. Sir Edmund Hillary, who, along with Sherpa Tenzing Norgay, was the first to summit Mt Everest and still epitomizes the "humble Kiwi hero" to many. They are proud both of his adventurous exploits and his quiet humanitarian efforts over many years in Nepal.

Other Kiwis who inspire adulation at home include movie producers Sir Peter Jackson and Fran Walsh, who put New Zealand on the map with the production of the *Lord of the Rings* and *Hobbit* trilogies, and more recently, Taika Waititi, who won Oscar acclaim with his satirical movie *Jojo Rabbit*.

Former prime minister Helen Clark continued her political career on the international stage, when she became the first woman to lead the United Nations Development Program. Kiwis particularly admire their sporting heroes, one of whom is sailor Sir Peter Blake. Sir Blake won the America's Cup for New Zealand in 1995 and 2000 only to be tragically killed the following year by pirates off the coast of Brazil while sailing to raise awareness about global warming. A more recent sporting hero is All Blacks rugby captain Richie McCaw. Under his leadership the national team have won back-to-back World Cup tournaments and today he is a role model for many young Kiwis.

REGIONAL RIVALRIES

In keeping with the theme of pride, there's a friendly but persistent rivalry between New Zealand's main regions, the most obvious being that between the North and South. Each island claims to have advantages over the other, though in many ways, they are quite different.

Two-thirds of New Zealand's population lives on the North Island. It has more cities and more diversity among the populations that reside in them. Auckland, for example, has the largest Polynesian population in the world. North Island city-dwellers, therefore, tend to see themselves as more cosmopolitan than those in the South. The North Island is also less mountainous and "tamer" than the South Island, with more arable land available for farming. The climate is warmer, too, and can grow crops like citrus and kiwifruit that South Islanders can only dream of. North Islanders sometimes joke about Invercargill—New Zealand's southernmost city—being cold enough for penguins to walk down the main street. Ironically, that joke was turned on its head in 2019 when two penguins popped up to feast on sushi scraps at a Wellington restaurant.

South Islanders, however, prefer their sparse population and mountainous setting. They call their island "The Mainland" and refer to themselves as "Mainlanders." There are just five cities on the South Island, and, because of the Southern Alps, which run down the island's center, fewer roads connect them. While many Maori *iwi* (clans) settled (and fought) in the North Island, one powerful *iwi*, Ngai Tahu, inhabits the South Island, and so there tend to be fewer Maori living south of Christchurch.

Overall, South Islanders are seen as more rural and perhaps more practical than their North Island cousins. One stereotype is the "Southern Man," laconic but ingenious—able to ride a horse, control a mob of cattle with just a whistle and a couple of dogs, and drink plenty of Speights (a brand of beer) in his spare time. In contrast, Nelson and Marlborough are seen as the sunny provinces, full of artists and hippies. You can still find both stereotypes on the South Island, but most Mainlanders see themselves as somewhere in between these two extremes.

A little less jovial is the rivalry between Auckland and the rest of the country. One-third of the country's population lives in Auckland and those outside see its inhabitants as harboring something of a big-city attitude and accuse them of being only interested in their own concerns. As with any stereotype, it may be true in part but it is by no means universal, especially considering the fact that many Aucklanders today hail from other parts of the country and indeed the world.

New Zealand's rural and small-town populations are different again. Farming and country people often have a "she'll be right" attitude and a "number eight wire" mentality. Number eight wire was a lightweight steel wire that was popular for its utility among Kiwi farmers in the nineteenth century—today it describes ingenuity, resourcefulness, and an ability to make do with what you have.

Many New Zealand towns like to advertise what they are best known for by displaying large, unusual sculptures or signs. So, you'll see enormous trout and salmon sculptures in Gore and Rakaia (known for their world-class fishing rivers) and a massive bottle in Paeroa (home of the iconic L&P fizzy drink). Cromwell—in the heart of Aotearoa's stone-fruit region—boasts gigantic fruit. Otohoranga (home of Kiwiana) has a rainbow-colored kiwi at each entrance to the town.

CLEAN AND GREEN

The Kiwis have a great love of the outdoors, and it shows. The names of local plants, trees, and birds are known to many, and most feel strongly about reducing greenhouse emissions, recycling, and combating climate change. The government too has taken up the issue with increasing urgency in recent years, and for good reason: from 2015 to 2019 New Zealand's glaciers melted at a rate that was seven times faster than just a decade earlier, a stark indication of rising temperatures. Other challenges include deteriorating waterways, increasing irrigation, and endangered animal species.

Before humans arrived, Aotearoa was a land of birds, reptiles, insects, and plants with just one mammal species: native bats. The Maori brought with them dogs, mice, and rats and introduced plants such as *kumara*, the sweet potato. They cleared and burned land for planting crops and hunted the largest birds, the Moa, to extinction. British settlers cleared even more land for farms. They introduced animals and plants, which quickly became invasive pests in their new land. For example, possums now destroy native bush and eat native birds' eggs and chicks, while rabbits have become the bane of many a farm and landowner. In addition, farmers wage a constant battle against gorse, broom, and thistles, and the government has invested millions of dollars into efforts to halt the spread of biodiversity-destroying wilding pines. Too late, Kiwis realized the errors of the past, and New Zealand now has stringent border controls for plants and animal products. Do not try to sneak food or plants into the country—if you're caught, the fines are severe. Worse is the genuine possibility of introducing yet another pest—usually insects or diseases in this modern age.

Today, the environmental situation remains comparatively good, even in urban areas, where more than 80 percent of Kiwis live: people don't need to wear masks because of air pollution; sewage is treated in ponds, not discharged straight into rivers or seas; and every district provides household collection and bins in public places for rubbish and recycling. New Zealand is a signatory to the Paris Climate Change Agreement and government plans to cut emissions include reducing fossil fuel use and production, promoting consumer migration to electric vehicles, planting trees, and researching and implementing ways to minimize animal, farm, and industrial emissions. As mentioned in the previous chapter, more than 80 percent of New Zealand's electricity is already sourced from renewable sources, and the government plans to increase that figure to 100 percent by 2035. Watch this space . . .

RELIGION

Christianity has had a profound effect on the development of New Zealand society.

It was first brought over by the British in the 1800s, when missionaries sought to tame the carousing whalers and to convert the Maori—this was despite Hongi Hika's statement that Christianity was no good as a religion for warriors! He was the Ngapuhi chief who, in 1820, was presented to the court of King George IV and showered with presents. He promptly sold these on his return to New Zealand for muskets, which he used to great effect against his enemies.

The Maori, of course, already had their own cultural and spiritual practices, with many gods and deities, often relating to the natural world (for example, Tane Mahuta, God of the Forest, and Tāwhirimātea, God of Wind and Storms). *Tohunga* (priests) communicated with *atua* (spirits), and *matakite* could see the future. Owing to the polytheistic nature of their beliefs, many tribes were willing to accommodate the God of the European settlers. This later gave birth to the Ratana and Ringatu movements, both Maori churches. Many Maori also became devout members of the other Christian denominations and have introduced a distinct Maori flavor to their practices.

The prominence of churches throughout New Zealand shows that Christianity is still very much part of the life of the country, although, following the world trend, congregations have shrunk, and the Church's influence has declined. According to the latest national census of 2018, some 36.5 percent of Kiwis identify as Christian, while almost half the country (48.2 percent) describe themselves as having no formal faith at all. There are also small Muslim, Jewish, Buddhist, and Hindu communities as a result of New Zealand's diverse immigrant population.

MARRIAGE AND FAMILY

While family structures vary according to ethnic, cultural, and religious influences, most New Zealanders are likely to be in a nuclear family, with extended family living separately. There is an emphasis on monogamy when you become a couple, and marriage is still a vital institution, despite the Church's waning influence. Couples, including same-sex couples, will often live together for several years before "tying the knot." Same-sex marriage has been legal in Aotearoa since 2013 and civil unions since 2005.

By and large, New Zealanders tend to marry for love rather than convenience or family ties. However, the divorce rate too is high, and as such, more and more couples are choosing to remain "de facto." De facto relationships are those longer than three years, whereby the couple live together and/or have a child together, but are not married nor in a civil union. Under these circumstances, couples are considered as though they are married in the eyes of the law, and the same laws concerning property division and child custody apply if they were to separate or one spouse were to die.

In Maori, the word for family is *whānau,* and it encompasses the whole extended family. Maori trace their family heritage through *hapu* and *iwi* (tribes) back to their traditional *waka* (the first canoe that each tribe's ancestors arrived on from Hawaiki). It is common among Maori, Polynesian, and Asian families for several generations to live together under one roof, or for their houses to be in close proximity.

Today, many New Zealanders choose to establish themselves in careers before having children, and as a result, the median age for women giving birth in 2017 has increased and is now at 30, compared to 25 in the 1970s. Family sizes vary between one to twelve or more children, but in the twenty-first century, it is more common for families to have two or three. There are more blended families, too, as adults form new partnerships later in life, with each having children from a previous relationship.

above oneself," with everyone being treated the same. Today, though social differences have emerged based on where people live and their occupations, they are not as pronounced as they are, say, in England, and there is no formal class structure.

Kiwis also generally see themselves as being open-minded toward change and new ideas, and most are proud of the country's liberal social attitudes. New Zealand was the first country in the world to give women the right to vote in 1893, and when the same-sex marriage bill came before parliament in 2013, the bill was passed by an overwhelming majority. LGBT people throughout New Zealand celebrated, and while some conservative groups disapproved, most Kiwis, especially younger people, thought it was about time. Overall, Kiwis are very accepting of the LGBT community and there are many openly gay people found throughout society, including in parliament. Trans people are more likely to meet bias, despite New Zealand being the first country in the world to elect a transgender mayor—and later MP—Georgina Beyer.

While progress has been made regarding gender representation in occupations, from engineering to nursing, a gender pay gap persists both within professions and between professions. In 2013, care and support worker Kristine Bartlett filed a claim under the Equal Pay Act, saying that her career was undervalued because it is traditionally carried out by women; the court upheld her complaint and the subsequent pay raise was passed on to other workers in the sector.

In 2019, the gender pay gap measured at 9.3 percent, down from 11.8 percent in 2015, and the government has introduced an accreditation system to further encourage corporations to improve pay equality among staff.

MANA AND RESPECT

Mana is a word that is often heard in Aotearoa. Its meaning is broad and includes prestige, authority, control, power, influence, status, spiritual power, and charisma, among other things. Kiwis, and especially Maori, believe that everyone has *mana*, which can be increased or diminished by their actions and how others treat them. The more *mana* a person has, the more respect they are likely to receive.

In general, Kiwis are big on respect and don't like to offend others if it can be avoided. For that reason, they often find it difficult to speak out publicly and may withhold their opinion. Similarly, many New Zealanders find it challenging to give an outright "no" to requests and so tend to be more indirect in their answers; "we'll see," "yeah-nah," and "yeah right!" (said sarcastically) can all mean no.

When it comes to conversation, New Zealanders like to keep things casual and are quick to use first names—even the current prime minister is more likely to be called Jacinda than Ms. Ardern.

Because Aotearoa has a relatively small population, people are used to having plenty of room and respect of one another's personal space is expected. On busy city streets, people will smile and greet the people they know, while in a small town people are more likely to acknowledge everyone they meet, at least with a smile or nod. In contrast to other Western countries, people in New Zealand are generally trusting of others, until they have reason not to be.

Joining the line and waiting your turn is considered basic manners in New Zealand, as is holding the door open for someone who needs help. Spitting in public is frowned upon, as is smoking indoors. By law all public buildings are smoke free and most provide outside spaces where people can go if they wish to smoke.

TALL POPPIES AND HUMBLE HEROES

New Zealanders like to celebrate other Kiwis, especially when they succeed overseas. That said, those that do find success are expected to be humble and even self-deprecating about their achievements, for if not they run the risk of being accused of "getting above themselves."

"Tall Poppy Syndrome," as it is otherwise known, is very real here, and when people's success elevates or distinguishes them, others can be envious and try to cut them down to size.

Many New Zealanders are trying to reduce what they see as being an unnecessarily negative attitude towards success; today, more media stories focus on celebrating success and achievement than in the past, while entrepreneurs, artists, actors, celebrities, and sportspeople have spoken out about the effect that hateful comments have had on their well-being and mental health. Schools routinely acknowledge their students' successes and through the national award system, people are honored for their contributions to New Zealand. Similarly, councils honor local citizens, and clubs award life memberships.

A land of volunteers

Many things wouldn't get done in Aotearoa if it weren't for its humble heroes—its countless volunteers. These people coach local sports teams. They run charity shops and hold fundraisers up and down the country. Volunteers set up and maintain food banks, man the rural fire service, and staff the Citizens Advice Bureau. Even the country's ambulance service is a charity, staffed by volunteers in the towns and rural areas too sparsely populated to warrant full-time paramedics.

CHAPTER THREE

CUSTOMS & TRADITIONS

MAORI CULTURE

Maori culture is an inextricable part of New Zealand's identity. As original inhabitants, they are known as *tangata whenua*, "people of the land." However, their name is derived from *Ma-Uri*, which means "children of Heaven." Maori comprise many *iwi* (tribes), *hapu* (subtribes), and *whanau* (extended family units). Originating in Polynesia, they brought the region's rich culture with them. Then, in adapting to the new land, they developed their own distinctive culture, passing on their history, myths, knowledge, and *whakapapa*, or "genealogies," through song, dance, art, and impassioned speeches as they had no written language.

The concepts of *mana* (see page 65) and *utu* (reciprocity, payment, or revenge) are central to Maori culture. *Mana* came from one's ancestors, who provided guidance and spiritual strength when called upon. Sometimes, that meant warfare and violence. Other times there was peace between tribes. People usually lived in unprotected *pa* (settlements) and seasonal camps. The *pa* initially resembled British Iron Age forts and later developed into more effective defences with trenches and pits. Today, the Department of Conservation manages around 10,000 *pa* sites, ranging from the earliest Polynesian settlements to nineteenth-century Maori economic, spiritual, and military sites. This is a key national collection, protected from avoidable harm and development pressures.

Maori Beliefs

The *tangata whenua's* relationship with the environment and belief in deities and *atua* helped the Maori to develop a system known as *tapu*, meaning "sacred" or "holy."

They had a strict division between things that were *tapu* and others that were *noa*, without sacred or holy power. For instance, cooked food was not permitted in sacred areas because it was *noa*.

In all matters, Maori believed in divine direction, a legacy from their Polynesian past, where religion is closely tied to nature and the environment around them. They have a rich store of myths and legends to explain the creation of the universe, its gods, and the people and animals that inhabit it.

Rangi (Sky Father) and Papatuanuku (Earth Mother) were parents to a host of deities, such as Tane, the god of trees and birds, Tawhiri, the god of winds, and Tangaroa, the god of the sea. All these gods are remembered through song and dance. There are many stories about

HOW THE KIWI LOST HIS WINGS

One day, so the story goes, Tane Mahuta, the lord of the forest, was surveying his ferny domain and became concerned that his children, the trees, were ill from being eaten by bugs. He called the birds together to ask if any might be prepared to eat the bugs, which would entail living on the dark, damp forest floor.

Not surprisingly, he was met with reluctance. Most preferred flying around in the sunny sky above. The *tui*'s excuse was that he was afraid of the dark, the *pukeko* didn't want to get his feet wet, and the *pipiwharauroa* was preoccupied with building a nest. But the Kiwi put himself forward.

Tane Mahuta reminded him that he would never see daylight again, he would lose all his beautiful feathers, and he would grow thick, strong legs, which he would need for ripping open the fallen trees. The Kiwi agreed to do the job, and as a reward for his sacrifice became the best-known and most-loved bird of all.

The other birds did not fare so well. The *tui* was forced to wear two white feathers on his throat as the mark of a coward, the *pukeko* would live forever in a swamp, and the *pipiwharauroa* would never have another nest of her own, but would have to lay her eggs in those of other birds.

the trickster Maui, about how he fished up New Zealand and tricked the goddess Mahuika out of all her fire. Another tale tells how stars came from the tears of Uru, the forgotten child of Rangi and Papa. In his sadness, Uru would weep, filling baskets with his tears. When his brother, Tane Mahuta, opened the baskets, they became dancing, bright lights, or *whetu*. Tane Mahuta scattered these all over the sky so that Uru would not be lonely in the dark.

Tohunga (priests) were very influential in the community. They communicated the gods' rules for living to the people and ensured that customs were observed correctly. They were both spiritual and physical healers and guided the rituals of hunting, fishing, and warfare. They raised the *tapu* of newly built *waka* or *whare* (houses) and during *tangi* (funerals).

RITUALS AND PROTOCOL

Tangihanga

Maori have a close relationship with their ancestors and so *tangihanga*, funerals, are hugely significant. Wakes continue for several days, with relatives and acquaintances attending from all over the country. The farewell to the dead includes rituals, songs, myths, and legends. In this way, Maori honor the dead and pass their genealogies and heritage on to the younger generation.

New Zealand's national rugby team, the All Blacks, performing the *haka*.

Haka

The *haka* is a challenging war dance and chant performed by a group of warriors. In former times, men performed a *haka* to test visitors' intentions. Rivals would be frightened by the warriors' might; others would prove they were coming in peace. *Haka* were also used before battle to prepare the warriors. Today, *haka* are performed on many occasions, from family, school, and sporting events to welcoming dignitaries. The New Zealand All Blacks rugby team perform their famous *haka* every time they contest an international match.

Marae

A *marae* is a fenced-in complex of carved buildings and grounds—including a *wharenui*, or meeting house, which is the focus of community identity and the place where all ceremonies are held. The *marae* is used for meetings, celebrations, funerals, educational workshops, and other important tribal events. Each *marae* belongs to a particular *iwi* (tribe), *hapū* (sub-tribe), or *whānau* (family), and Maori see their *marae* as *tūrangawaewae*—their place to stand and belong. *Marae* have a strict, formal protocol, called a *powhiri*, whereby visitors are welcomed into the

The interior of the *marae* at Waitangi National Reserve, North Island.

marae. Each *marae* has its own *tapu* (see page 70), and strangers must wait to be invited in.

The *powhiri* begins with the *wero*, or challenge, when a traditionally dressed warrior, complete with *taiaha* (spear), will lay down a token for the guests to pick up, to indicate their peaceful intentions. Then comes a *karanaga*, a high-pitched woman's call, which brings the *manuhiri* (visitors) onto the *marae*. Inside the *whare runanga* there are speeches of welcome and response, ceremonial chants and songs from hosts and visitors, who may also give a *koha* or gift. Finally, the hosts and visitors exchange a *hongi* (sharing of breath), where two people gently press noses and breathe in at the same time.

ETIQUETTE

It is essential to understand that some Maori sites are *tapu*, particularly burial grounds, and should not be touched. Before entering the *marae*, remove your footwear. Don't smoke, eat, drink, or chew gum in the *wharenui*, or sit on tables, or any surface where food is prepared or eaten. Don't take photographs of buildings unless you have express permission. The *marae* is an important and sacred part of Maori life and its rules and traditions should be respected.

ART FORMS

Maori have a significant tradition of carving important wooden buildings and canoes, and fashioning *pounamu* (greenstone) into tools and ornaments. The decorative carvings reflect the deep respect in which ancestors are held. Art forms include carved walking sticks, engravings on bone, and *pounamu* necklaces, all important because they carry the original owners' spirit. There are also carvings and panels showing the *whakapapa* (genealogy) and history of the *iwi* (tribe) on every *marae*.

Despite Western influence and the fact that more than 500,000 Maori now live in cities, they retain a vital connection to their *iwi* and *marae*.

Rituals and ceremonies still use the traditional music and dance, and Maori traditions and art forms have become *taonga,* or national treasures. At the same time, Maori artists bring their culture into the twenty-first century by creating modern songs in Te Reo.

Tattoos

Since 1500 BC, tattooing has been an integral part of the Tahitian culture from which Maori originated. When they came to Aotearoa, ancient Maori developed a distinct style of tattooing called *tamoko*. The word "tattoo" itself derives from the Tahitian *tatau*, meaning "open wound." While today tattoos are popular worldwide, *moko* are much more than a decoration. They illustrate tribal affiliations and origins, family, social status, and *mana*. An older, high-status man would have a full face, complex *moko*, while a younger man may only have a few tattoos.

Maori have a legend about how a handsome young chief called Mataora brought *moko* into the world. He had fallen in love with and married a spirit from the underworld. One day she fled after Mataora hit her, so he followed her to the underworld. There he discovered the art of *tamoko* and brought it back to the land of the living.

Originally *moko* were applied with a wood carving technique. The carver dipped a chisel-like bone in a pigment made from the soot of burnt candlenut mixed with water and oil. Then, he used a wooden stick to tap the bone against the skin, so puncturing it. Today

artists use a machine developed from an electric shaver to eliminate the risk of disease. Tattoo designs were like those used in other Maori art forms, with many designs taken from nature. Only men could have a full-face *moko*, while women tattooed the chin, upper lip, and nostrils.

Sometimes the right to bear a specific tattoo had to be earned. In older days, it was said that a man without a *moko* was a *papatea*, or "plain face," meaning a nobody. Full-face *moko* were discouraged by the British, and the practice all but died out by the 1920s. Maori artists began to reclaim *tamoko* in the 1970s and 80s. Today, *moko* are an increasingly seen and accepted part of mainstream New Zealand.

OTHER INFLUENTIAL CULTURES

British

While Britain settled both New Zealand and Australia, it is New Zealand today that more readily acknowledges its British ancestry. At the turn of the twentieth century, it was still very British, with 20 percent of its population born in the UK; now that figure is closer to 6 percent. New Zealand still feels quite strongly about the Queen, still celebrates her official birthday, and has not taken any steps down the Republican route, as Australia has. The United Kingdom, especially London, is often the first stop for most young Kiwis on their "overseas experience," otherwise known as "the big OE," an extended trip for twenty-somethings that has become a rite of passage in recent years.

British immigrants came to New Zealand from varying backgrounds and at different times, bringing their values with them, along with pies, fish and chips, and democracy; tastes and values that have stuck! The British brought with them traditions and customs too, as well as associations and organizations such as fire brigades, local militia, building societies, brass bands, and the friend societies, which helped the sick or bereaved before the Social Security Act of 1938. They played a prominent part in trade union activity, and contributed to the beginnings of the Labour Party.

Beer, which is still New Zealand's most popular alcoholic drink, was first brewed commercially in the country by a Londoner Joel Polack, who founded a brewery at Russell. Speights beer owes its origin to Yorkshireman James Speight, who, with partners from Devon and Scotland, started a brewery in Dunedin. Today, though, Kiwis usually ask for lagers served cold rather than the warm beer preferred by the early British settlers.

British TV programs such as *Downton Abbey* and *Coronation Street* are favorites, though today many American programs and reality shows have become popular too. New Zealand has Britain to thank for its church music, Christmas carols, and musical events such as the Proms music festival and concerts in the parks. The annual "A&P," agricultural and pastoral shows, come from the traditional British country shows. Since they began in the 1840s, they have evolved from being an opportunity for farmers to showcase their stock and produce and compete for prizes, to include a wide variety of entertainment. The shows usually last over a weekend or longer and include equestrian events and activities such as woodcutting contests, arts and crafts, and entertainment for children, making it a good outing for the whole family.

Many of the sports played in New Zealand are of British origin too. Soccer has gained in popularity, particularly since the Second World War, when more enthusiasts arrived from Britain. It had been slow to take off because few immigrants to the new country came from the Midlands area of England, where soccer originated. Horse racing has developed in the country, with the first formal meeting being held at the Bay of Islands in 1835. Today New Zealand thoroughbreds are valued worldwide for their superior bloodstock.

Early architecture also reflects British influence, and the 1850s saw buildings erected reminiscent of what had been left behind. Remnants of the Gothic revival style, as designed by English architects Benjamin Mountfort and Frederick Thatcher, can still be seen in a few older colonial homes, or "villas," as they are called locally.

Chinese

In the 1860s, Gabriel Read found gold in Central Otago, and within months the goldfields were inundated with hopeful miners. When gold was discovered further north, many European miners left Otago to make new claims. So, the Dunedin Chamber of Commerce recruited men from China's southeastern Guangdong province, reasoning that they would be hardworking and eventually return to their homeland. South China at the time was beset by overpopulation, shortage of land, famine, drought, banditry, and peasant revolts. That meant many men were willing to leave and seek their fortunes. Their wives remained at home, caring for older parents, and the men sent money home whenever they could. But as more men arrived, European settlers became fearful, and the Chinese faced increasing discrimination and hardship. From 1881 to 1944, the government imposed a "poll tax" on each Chinese person who entered the country. Initially £10 (equivalent to US $1200 in 2021), the tax was later raised to £100 (US $14,000 today). In addition, harsh laws were brought about to further discourage the inflow of Chinese citizens. For example, the Chinese were denied a pension until 1936, and naturalization only became legal in 1952.

It was during the Second World War that attitudes began to shift; China was fighting alongside Allied forces against Japan, and the government allowed groups of Chinese women to enter New Zealand as refugees. Many Chinese had become excellent market gardeners, too, and people appreciated the food that they grew.

By the 1980s and 90s, sentiment had changed markedly, and the government began to actively encourage the immigration of Chinese investors. The subsequent influx reinvigorated Chinese culture in New Zealand, as well as the local economy. Finally, in 2002, the government officially apologized to the Chinese community for the discrimination and suffering caused by the poll tax.

In the 2020s, restaurants representing different Chinese cuisines can be found throughout New Zealand, while specialist grocery shops sell ingredients for traditional dishes. Chinese developers fund many big projects, and, importantly, China is now New Zealand's biggest partner in trade. Chinese New Year festival events are held each January, while lantern festivals and dragon boat racing are popular, especially in Auckland, where most Chinese Kiwis live today.

Relations with Australia

Kiwis and "Aussies" have a love-hate relationship, rather like siblings who squabble but have each other's back when it matters. In the past, Australians would stereotype Kiwis as "hicks," and thought of them as provincial, while New Zealanders in return thought Aussies to be of "inferior stock" due to their convict origins. Aussies also used to call Kiwis "South Seas Poms," because of the country's close relationship with Britain.

Today, New Zealand's relationship with Australia—from an economic, social, and security viewpoint—is one of its most important. Until recently, Australia was New Zealand's largest market and strongest trading partner, and the two countries have similar foreign and trading policies. The Trans-Tasman arrangement of 1973 between the two countries allowed for free movement across the Tasman Sea, with each nationality being allowed to live and work in the other country without restrictions, although, in reality, fewer Australians took advantage of this. Consequently, those Kiwis choosing to live in Australia were often accused of taking Aussie jobs or living off welfare benefits, although, since 2001, New Zealanders are barred from applying for citizenship and denied access to an ever-increasing number of government services. New Zealanders often complain that the Aussies poach New Zealand's best brains, and many Oz headhunting agencies recruit Kiwi medical and educational professionals, and also members of the New Zealand police force.

A joining of the two countries has in the past been raised, but, ever since New Zealand declined to become Australia's seventh state in 1901, opinion polls have shown that New Zealanders are still totally against the idea.

Nevertheless, the two nations have much in common, including their former colonial ties with England and their inheritance of the British system of government, their support of Britain during two world wars, their alignment with the US during the Cold War, participation in both the Korean and Vietnam Wars, and their relative isolation from the rest of the world. While their relationships with Britain have declined into more of a love–hate affair, Australia is far more republican than New Zealand, which continues to support the monarchy. More recently, in 1999, both countries were involved with the UN in the peacekeeping force for East Timor, though it was only Australia that went to war in the 2003 invasion of Iraq.

It is on the playing field, however, that the rivalry comes to the surface, particularly in cricket and rugby, the two games that have become part of each nation's identity. Australian cricket captain Trevor Chappell's "unsportsmanlike" underarm delivery on the final ball in 1981, for instance, has never been forgiven by New Zealand's cricket enthusiasts. However, beyond the traditional rivalry and differences of opinion, Kiwis and Aussies still defend one another abroad, as Antipodeans against the rest. Put them on the rugby field though, and it's game on.

NATIONAL COLORS AND SYMBOLS

Since 1902 the New Zealand flag has a royal blue background, a Union Jack in the top left corner and features four red stars which represents the Southern Cross constellation to illustrate the country's location in the South Pacific Ocean. In 2016, New Zealanders were offered the chance to change their flag, but most voted against the proposed replacement.

Maori have several flags. The Tino Rangatiratanga flag is considered the national Maori flag: it is black and red and features a long white *koru*, symbolizing Te Ao Mārama, the "realm of being and light."

Aotearoa has several unofficial emblems too. They include the kiwi bird, the *kowhai* yellow flower, and the all-important silver fern frond from an endemic tree fern species.

The national colors are black and white or silver. National sports teams' uniforms are commonly either black or white, usually with a silver fern logo, and explain the names New Zealand teams often adopt: the All Blacks men's national rugby team, the All Whites soccer team, the Tall Blacks basketball team, and the Black Sticks hockey team. Women's national teams are often named after the fern, as for example with the Silver Ferns netball team, the White Ferns cricket team, and the Black Ferns rugby team.

Red ochre is the little-known third national color and is found on national medals and decorations such as the Queens Service Medal and the New Zealand Order of Merit.

PUBLIC HOLIDAYS

New Zealand celebrates twelve cultural, national, and religious holidays. Many businesses close on public holidays, and those who must work receive extra wages (usually "time and a half"). Individual workers also receive a minimum of 20 days' paid annual leave, which often increases the longer they remain at their place of work.

Three national days have particular significance:

Waitangi Day (National Day)

New Zealanders celebrate their national day on February 6 with festivities in all cities and most towns. The most significant celebration is held at the Waitangi Treaty Grounds. The day begins with a dawn ceremony and flag raising, followed by breakfast, an interdenominational church service, and a 21-gun salute at noon. Music and dance acts from many cultures perform during the afternoon as festivalgoers enjoy the many food stalls,

Celebrations at the Waitangi Treaty Grounds mark the signing of New Zealand's national treaty in 1840.

markets, and children's activities. February 5 and 6 are also often a time of protest when Maori groups highlight important and sometimes contentious issues that are still to be addressed.

Anzac Day

Held on April 25, Anzac Day has a more somber and reflective mood. Initially, the day marked the Australia and New Zealand Army Corps' fateful landing at Gallipoli in 1915. Now the day commemorates all those who served in New Zealand's wars, conflicts, and peacekeeping operations. Every city and town hold one or more Anzac Day services—usually at dawn, where people gather at local memorials to attend marches by returned service personnel and to hear hymns, speeches, and prayers recited. Traditionally a bugler plays "Last

Post," and the fourth verse of Laurence Binyon's poem "For the Fallen" is read.

Matariki (Maori New Year)

The Maori New Year falls in late June, which is winter in the Southern Hemisphere. It celebrates the first rising of the Pleiades star cluster, which Maori call Matariki, and signals the start of the Maori lunar calendar. Matariki is a time to gather with family and friends, reflect and celebrate the past, present, and future. Although it has been unofficially celebrated since ancient times, Matariki became Aotearoa's twelfth official public holiday in 2022.

OTHER PUBLIC HOLIDAYS

New Zealand also celebrates:

January 1 & 2 – New Year

March or April – Good Friday, Easter Sunday & Monday

1st Monday in June – Queen's Birthday

4th Monday in October – Labour Day

December 25 – Christmas Day

December 26 – Boxing Day

Each region in New Zealand has one additional regional anniversary day. These are spread throughout the year, beginning with Wellington's holiday in January and finishing with the Chatham Islands Day in November.

CHAPTER FOUR

MAKING FRIENDS

New Zealanders are open and welcoming to visitors but can be rather reserved about admitting new friends into their social circles and so, in general, it's easier to make casual friends and acquaintances than it is to form close friendships. Close friendships can be won, however; time and effort is required, but it is worthwhile. Your Kiwi friends will be reliable, honest, and there to help out should you need.

In general, Kiwis see themselves as progressive and accepting of differences. At the same time, they often resent those who show arrogance or boast about their achievements. As a result, even confident Kiwis tend to keep quiet about their most significant achievements.

MEETING AND GREETING

Greetings in New Zealand are casual and friendly. It's usual to smile, say hello, and shake hands when you first meet someone, especially if you're a man. Women don't always shake hands, but there is no reason not to offer a handshake regardless of gender. Closer physical greetings depend on familiarity and people's personal comfort levels; New Zealanders can often feel uncomfortable when people get too close and so hugging and kissing is less common in New Zealand than in some countries. Women tend to hug their friends, and men and women will embrace if they haven't met for a while, but it is rare for men to hug each other.

New Zealanders are big on using first names; it's unusual for someone to be introduced as "Mr." or "Ms." unless the setting is formal. For example, a doctor in a hospital, or PhD in a university, would be presented as Dr. but otherwise expect to be introduced with your first name and possibly surname. You'll hear many different greetings used in New Zealand in all sorts of languages. Some of the most common include gidday, how are you?

Kia ora (pronounced key-or-ah), and *morena* (more-en-ah), which means good morning.

The Maori ritual greeting is called a *hongi (hong-ee.)* Two people press their noses and foreheads together while holding one hand and putting the other hand on the shoulder. You are unlikely to use this greeting unless you are being welcomed onto a *marae*.

Generally, wherever you're trying to meet people, you will have to make the first move because Kiwis can be uncomfortable when approaching people they don't know. Start by saying "hi," with a smile, and then you can begin by chatting about the weather, the place, or whatever's happening around you. Be friendly and willing to contribute to the conversation or group and you will be off to a good start.

GETTING TO KNOW YOU

As in many countries, New Zealanders tend to form their main friendship circles in school and university, while new friendships can be found at work, and groups where people share the same interests or circumstances.

When you move to a new place, it can be challenging to break into those close-knit circles. Most "newbies" find themselves making friends with other expats rather than locals, at least to start with. Couples with a Kiwi/non-Kiwi pairing are more likely to be genuinely friendly than an all-Kiwi couple. Look out for others who are new to your area and actively searching for friendships too.

With that in mind, there are a number of ways to meet people and make new friends in New Zealand. If you're only in the country for a short time or are traveling around, you'll often find that older people are more likely to chat with you and sometimes even invite you for a meal. If you're backpacking and staying in hostels, you'll likely spend most of your time with other travelers, which can limit your exposure to local life.

If you're working in New Zealand, your workplace is an excellent place to meet other people and you will find your colleagues open to socializing. Companies often encourage social activities, including sports teams and Friday drinks with colleagues after work.

Hobby and interest groups are another way that Kiwis socialize. In most towns there are plenty of groups and clubs for all sorts of interests and activities, including sports, culture, service, religion, and friendship clubs, all of which provide an excellent way to meet people if you are in New Zealand for anything longer than a short trip.

If you are Christian, going to church is another place where friends can be made. Some congregations disperse quickly after a service, but others have time for socializing after services, when they will have tea and chat together. People will often be interested in and curious about where you come from, what life is like in your country, and (most importantly) what you think of New Zealand. (Tip: be complimentary!) Churches will have Bible study and outreach groups to join if you're staying in the area and want to get involved. Besides Christian churches, which are found in all towns and cities, larger centers have mosques, synagogues, and temples, too, especially on the North Island.

If you have kids, it's often much easier to integrate into a new place. For starters, you will meet other parents through preschool or school activities. Helping at after-school groups like Scouts, Guides, dance class, Kapa Haka (Maori cultural group), or kids' sports teams is another idea. Striking up a conversation with fellow parents at the playground is also fair game, especially if your children are of a similar age.

GOING OUT

New Zealand has a massive café culture, and it's common for people to go out for coffee or a meal together, especially after a shared experience like playgroup, gym class, or a meeting. Similarly, people will frequently meet at the pub for drinks over lunch or in the evening. Drinking alcohol here is not necessary as there will be many drinks available, including coffee, tea, and other non-alcoholic drinks.

Food is also an essential part of the Kiwi socializing culture. Smaller workplaces often celebrate birthdays with a shared morning tea. People meet for picnics in parks and at the beach. Maori will "put down a *hangi*" (a traditional ground pit oven) for all sorts of gatherings, from birthdays to funerals, and many summer and autumn events will include a barbecue. Invite new friends to go with you when you plan an outing to the beach or park for a picnic or a barbecue. You'll often get to know people better when you have something to do together on neutral ground.

In all these scenarios, don't expect to have deep conversations with your new Kiwi friends, at least not at first. Men, especially, tend to shy away from talking about their feelings or frustrations. That can be challenging for men who are from more open cultures.

HOSPITALITY

Many Kiwis keep their homes private and don't often invite people around. However, others are more welcoming and host dinners, parties, and barbeques. Board games and card evenings are popular in some circles, and friends will get together to play in the evenings. (If board games are your bag, check out the Counter Culture café in Wellington where friends and groups meet to play one of the hundreds of games on offer.) Another option is to take the initiative and invite people around to your house first.

Barbecues can range from informal sausages and bread at the beach to full-on feasts of steak, chicken kebabs, corn, and salads. It is usual to ask if you can contribute some meat or a salad, and bring a bottle of wine or some beer, even if the answer's no. Your host will have some drinks on hand, including non-alcoholic ones, but guests usually contribute too. In that case, you can drink what you've brought or put it on a drinks table to share. If you're invited to a dinner party, celebration, movie, or games night, again, bring wine, chocolates, or flowers, though they are a less common gift.

You may be invited to a potluck tea and asked to "bring a plate." That does not mean your hosts are running short of crockery! Rather, it means that everyone contributes to the meal by bringing a dish of food. All the food is set out on a table, and everyone is invited to help themselves. Ask what sort of "plate" your hosts would like so that everyone doesn't end up bringing the same thing. A bottle of wine makes for a good alternative gift if food isn't required.

When it comes to meal invitations, it is worth noting some of the terminology. If you are invited for afternoon tea, this will usually be between 3:00 and 4:00 p.m. and will be a cup of tea or coffee served with cakes, crackers, or cookies. If you are invited for tea, or dinner, you've been invited to an evening meal. Kiwis traditionally eat early—about 6:00 to 8:00 p.m. Supper is a later evening snack, usually held as part of an evening get-together or party.

DATING IN NEW ZEALAND

Both men and women ask each other out on a date in New Zealand. A good first date might be going out to dinner, the beach, a bar, or a party. It's perfectly acceptable to do this as part of a group, too.

Most students and young people socialize by going to bars, parties, and nightclubs. Kiwis love sporting events, but they tend to go as families or in a group and so they are not a good choice for a date. If you ask someone out to dinner for two, that implies you want to be alone and it might lead to physical intimacy later. Some New Zealanders are quite casual when it comes to sex and are likely to have several partners before settling down with one person. However, there are many different attitudes, and you should never assume that agreement to a date means someone will want to be intimate.

As elsewhere, New Zealanders have embraced online dating. They use several apps and websites to connect with other people looking for love, friendship, or maybe just a fling. Tinder, Bumble, Hinge, and Grindr are popular, while local dating websites include NZ Dating and FindSomeone.co.nz.

CLUBS AND SOCIETIES

Joining a club or society is a good and easy way to meet New Zealanders. Here is a list of different interest groups available to join:

Social Clubs and **Returned Service Association (RSA):** found in many large towns throughout NZ. Members have access to large social club rooms with bars & restaurants, pool tables, Sports TVs, card nights, etc.

Tertiary Education Student Associations: provide sport, support, social interaction, and clubs of all sorts.

Interests & Hobbies clubs: Stamps, photography, pottery, painting, quilting, caving, tramping, running, floral, gardening, climbing… whatever the interest, you can be sure that Kiwis have a club for it.

Sports Clubs: from athletics to yachting and (almost) every letter in between.

Rural Clubs: Rural Women, Young Farmers, Women's Institute.

Service Clubs: Rotary, MENZ sheds, Lions, Roundtable, Kiwanis.

Churches, Fellowship clubs: e.g. Probus.

Kids & Schools: including Youth clubs, Trampoline & other sports clubs, after school clubs, church clubs, PTAs, dance, drama or music lessons, Guides, and Scouts.

Charities: St Johns, Red Cross, World Vision, Variety Club, etc.

Activist/Interest Groups: Greenpeace, Forest and Bird, Amnesty International, Sustainable Coastlines.

Volunteering opportunities are available in a wide variety of charity and community organizations. See www.seekvolunteer.co.nz for ideas. Other groups include Newcomers Network, ethnic community groups, expat clubs and workplace social groups.

CHAPTER FIVE

THE KIWIS AT HOME

HOUSING

In times gone by, every Kiwi wanted to own the house they lived in. Most houses were on substantial grounds and New Zealand was known as "the quarter-acre pavlova paradise." Today, that dream is beyond the means of many households. In 2021, approximately 30 percent of New Zealand's families lived in rented homes while around 60 percent were homeowners. The majority of homeowners now are over the age of 50 and will have bought their properties decades ago, when house prices were more affordable. Low incomes in some sectors of the population, changes to tax laws, and rising house prices have all contributed to New Zealand's falling homeownership rates.

In 2019, experts warned that rising house prices were signs of a housing crisis that had been years in the making. Then, Covid-19 struck and the subsequent spike in the number of Kiwis returning home placed further pressure on the already limited housing stock, causing house prices to soar.

The average house price in Auckland in 2021 was NZ $1,207,860, (roughly US $880,000), while the country-wide median was NZ $730,000 (US $530,000). However, housing costs vary from region to region, and in some rural or isolated areas, houses are much cheaper (usually because they are further from jobs and amenities). Mortgage rates in 2021 averaged around 3 percent per annum, with most households electing for fixed rate rather than floating loans. At least two-thirds of privately owned dwellings are mortgaged.

Many students, single people, and couples in New Zealand often "go flatting" in their younger years, sharing a house or apartment with others. Maori and Pacific Islanders are also more likely to live in rented accommodation. At the same time, Kiwis of Asian and European descent more often own their own homes. More than three-quarters of New Zealanders live in urban areas of at least 10,000 people, and just 16.3 percent live rurally.

The New Zealand government provides state houses for many people who cannot afford to own homes or rent from private landlords. Over the years, this housing program has been heavily influenced by governmental policy. As elsewhere, the center-right wing governments tended towards less state intervention and more private enterprise. Consequently, the National-led governments of the 1990s and 2000s introduced market-rental rates in

State housing. They also sold many houses when they subsequently became vacant because their tenants could no longer afford the rent. The current Labour-led and left-leaning government aims to reverse the trend, linking rents to incomes rather than market rates and providing more social housing. In the 2020s, the Labour government pledged to build thousands of modern, warm, and dry state homes. They also initiated the Kiwi Build program to encourage developers to build more affordable privately owned houses, and introduced a range of measures to cool the market and boost supply; time will tell to what extent these policies will succeed in providing affordable and sufficient housing for all New Zealanders.

Architecture and Housing Styles

While much of New Zealand's architecture has been influenced by overseas trends, it also has many award-winning architects who developed something of a local style. (See for example John Scott, whose buildings uniquely combined Maori and contemporary design elements, or Chris Moller, the long-time presenter of New Zealand's *Grand Designs* TV show and creator of the Click-Raft prefab building system.)

Today, most private dwellings are detached homes for one family, but multiunit homes and apartments are increasing, mainly due to lack of space. You can often tell when a New Zealand house was built by its style. In the early twentieth century, Kiwis tended to build single-story wooden villas and bungalows. After the

A family home in Auckland, North Island.

Second World War, houses became more restrained and box-like. The 1970s saw Kiwis branch out with "colonial," "ranch," "Mediterranean," and "contemporary" styles. But in the 1990s, standards dropped and new building materials were introduced. Subsequently, it emerged that many houses were not watertight and resulted in the great "leaky homes" crisis, which saw thousands of structures having to be repaired or rebuilt.

Building standards have since markedly improved. Insulation is mandatory, and eco-building, which favors energy efficiency, is encouraged. Modern homes usually have between two and four bedrooms, two bathrooms, and are often two or three stories high. Another current trend is for transportable homes, constructed off-site and trucked to their destination. Tiny houses are also growing in popularity; these can be an affordable and eco-friendly way for people to own their first home.

Compared to many countries, much of New Zealand's housing stock is young and recently built. A few impressive nineteenth-century houses remain, however, and some are open to visitors. You can ask at the local i-SITE Visitor Information Centres about historic homes in the area if you are interested. Unfortunately, the Christchurch earthquake in 2011 destroyed many heritage buildings and houses. Some, like the Arts Centre, the Lyttelton Timeball Tower, and the iconic Christchurch Cathedral are being rebuilt. Many others were irreparably damaged. As a result, many cities and towns are now working to strengthen their heritage buildings.

Oamaru, in the South Island, is well known for the beautiful buildings in its heritage area near the harbor. Napier, which was destroyed by an earthquake in 1931, is now famous for its art deco style. The tiny town of Kawakawa in Northland boasts an impressive Hundertwasser-designed public toilet block. And in Wellington you can find examples of almost every major architectural style of the last 150 years, from simple wooden houses to curving, vibrant postmodern structures.

The "Bach"

Many New Zealanders have a vacation home, commonly called a "bach" in most of the country and a "crib" in Otago and Southland. Traditionally, a bach was a basic shelter, usually made of cheap materials, such as recycled timber and corrugated iron. The name

A humble West Coast bach; it's really all you need.

is short for "bachelor pad" and comes from early, men-only fishing trips, when they only needed the essentials. Many early bachs were erected illegally on beaches. Others popped up in the remote backcountry, beside lakes and mountains, in fact, in any beautiful spot.

The original bachs had rainwater tanks and primitive lavatories known as "dunnies" or "long drops." Nowadays, many new bachs are architect-designed and have lost the original "make-do" character, though you will still find clusters of well-used bachs and cribs in the less upmarket spots.

The Shed

Many "good Kiwi blokes" (and gals) are practical do-it-yourselfers, and they love their sheds and workshops. Here they will mend anything from cars to lawnmowers, or tinker with models and inventions. So great is the tradition of the shed that there is even a society dedicated to it. MENZSHED, set up in 2013, is a space for people (women are accepted at some "sheds" too!) to come together, share skills, have a laugh, and work together either on personal or group projects.

Garage Sales

When Kiwis are moving house or want to clear out some space, they will often hold a garage sale; after all, one man's junk is another man's treasure. Furniture, toys, and clothing will be stacked and arranged in the garage for all to come and peruse.

They are usually held on a Saturday morning and advertised in the local newspaper and on the Internet, often listing the major items on offer. Regular sellers are careful to add the words "not before [a certain time]" in their advertisement to stop bargain hunters from arriving too early. Many people go from one sale to another, even just to see what the neighbors are throwing out. Still, garage sales can be a valuable source for those wanting to buy cheap second-hand goods.

"Shifting" and "Going Walkabout"

New Zealanders move or, as they term it, "shift" a lot. The average Kiwi moves every five years and it is not unusual to see several realtors in even a small town.

They also love to holiday in and explore their own country, often in a mobile home. New Zealanders tow caravans (trailers), drive campervans (RVs) and even convert buses into sophisticated homes on wheels complete with wood-burning fires, microwaves, and TV. A few months' break often lengthens into a few years, and such travelers have formed their own club with groups of "roadies," as they call themselves, meeting up regularly at favorite spots throughout the country.

Local rules on "Freedom Camping"—the parking of a camper by a lake or a river—vary in each area of New Zealand. While it was once easy to park anywhere, visitors often left trash, or worse, which polluted the area and annoyed the locals. That led to regional councils tightening the rules with some banning Freedom Camping altogether. However, there are many designated camping grounds throughout Aotearoa. As well as parking, they also have communal kitchens and ablution blocks, grass, trees, and playgrounds. If you prefer a "back to nature" experience, the Department of Conservation provides basic camping grounds in many remote areas. These have toilets and barbecue areas and a very reasonable nightly charge.

EDUCATION

New Zealand has a four-tier education system, allowing people of all ages to gain formal skills and qualifications.

Early Childhood (ECE)

While preschool education is not compulsory, 95 percent of New Zealand children under five will attend some form of early childhood education, usually for twenty to twenty-two hours a week. For three- and four-year-olds, the first twenty hours per week are fully funded by the government. ECE includes daycares, Montessori centers, kindergartens, and play centers. Staff usually have formal qualifications. There are also informal playgroups throughout the country and home-based care programs such as Barnardos.

Primary School

It is compulsory to start primary school by six years old, but many New Zealand children begin at five. Most schools have a transition class to bring their younger students from the play-based ECE curriculum into the more academic primary system.

Officially, primary school children are classed as Years One to Eight (aged five–twelve or thirteen). The curriculum covers a broad range, from reading, writing, and math through science, social sciences, technology, and the arts, languages, and digital technology. From 2022 it will be compulsory to teach New Zealand history, with an emphasis on local history.

Secondary School

The word college in New Zealand doesn't refer to a university. Instead, a college or high school is for students aged between twelve and eighteen, in Years 9–13. High schools focus on broad education for their younger students and specialize as students move into Years 11–13.

Secondary education includes plenty of opportunities for participation in sport, the arts, clubs, and social events and fosters teenagers' growing maturity. Almost all secondary schools and many primary schools require their students to wear a school uniform.

Tertiary Education

New Zealand has a wide range of tertiary education options with state and private providers in each of the main centers with satellite campuses in smaller areas. Options include eight world-class universities and three Maori-focused institutions called *wananga* which offer a broad spectrum of higher studies to Master's level, working from a Maori perspective. The NZ Institute of Skills and Technology has campuses throughout the country, while other organizations train in specific industry sectors.

Aotearoa's adult education also has many flexible options, such as distance learning, night school, and part-time study. It is quite common for adults in New Zealand to return to tertiary study to improve their qualifications while they are working or to change careers later in life.

In the System

State primary schools are usually coeducational, as are many secondary schools. Each school is governed by a board of trustees elected by the parents. Schools are inspected every three to five years to ensure they meet strict standards. Education is free for pupils from five to nineteen years of age and compulsory between six and sixteen. However, many state schools do ask parents to contribute to school expenses.

The school day for primary students usually starts at 9:00 a.m. and finishes at 3:00 p.m.; secondary schools start earlier and finish later. The school year runs from February to December and has four terms. Each term is roughly ten weeks long. Summer holidays last about five and a half weeks at primary schools and about a

The University of Otago in Dunedin, South Island.

week longer at secondary schools. The autumn, winter, and spring holidays each last two weeks, and schools also observe the public holidays when they fall during term time.

The tertiary academic year has two semesters, commencing in February and finishing in November. Universities often run summer schools as well. Teacher education is offered at colleges of education, some universities, and private training institutions. Students contribute to fees for most courses, but a loan scheme makes higher education more easily accessible. New Zealand attracts many overseas students, particularly those from Southeast Asia, as international education has become a significant source of export earnings.

Most Maori are educated within the state system, but there are also Maori immersion schools (Kura Kaupapa), where the Maori language is preserved, and education is based on Maori culture and traditional values. Some early childhood education centers are aligned with certain cultures, such as Maori, Chinese, or Pasifika. Te Kōhanga Reo, for example, emphasizes the use of Maori language and practices.

Numeracy and literacy continue to be significant issues in education. International statistics reveal that the gap between New Zealand's best and worst achievers is greater than anywhere else in the developed world. Still, in 2018 New Zealand students performed well above average in the latest OECD Program for International Student Assessment (PISA).

The National Certificate of Educational Achievement is the graduation qualification acquired at secondary level. Students can gain NCEA at three levels, which correspond to the last three years of secondary schooling. It is awarded when a certain number of credits have been achieved; university qualification requires forty-two credits, for example.

Subjects are assessed internally (through assignments) and externally (through exams and portfolios), and students are encouraged to aim for "excellence." The change from the previous exam-based qualifications was designed to allow students to show the breadth of their learning, not merely answer the questions asked in exams.

DAILY LIFE

The vast majority of New Zealanders go to work or school, spend time with their families and friends, and complete daily activities such as housework and sleeping. Many are involved in outdoor or other leisure activities. They play sports, volunteer in the community, look after their children, watch TV, and surf the Internet of course.

Some families and ethnic communities are very church-focused, so a lot of their time is spent on church activities. Others tinker in their sheds and backyards, go biking on the many cycle trails, or hiking in the mountains or bush. Still more New Zealanders enjoy getting out onto the water.

Work-life

Office jobs and many factory and shop jobs in Aotearoa usually start between 8:00 and 9:00 a.m. and finish at 5:00 p.m. Those who work in the cities but live in the suburbs face the dreaded "rush hour" traffic morning and evening, as everyone scrambles to drive to work at the same time. Others catch the bus, walk, or cycle to work. Only Wellington and Auckland have commuter trains and regular ferry services. In the smaller cities and towns, rush hour is far less of a hassle. Traffic will be busier than usual but not brought to a standstill, nor continue for two or more hours, as it does in Auckland, Wellington, and Christchurch.

Legally, staff must be able to take a paid ten-minute break in the morning and afternoon. Lunchtime varies from thirty–sixty minutes and is unpaid. Usually, city and factory workers will buy food from a café or sandwich bar or bring their lunch from home. Business meetings are often held over a coffee or lunch in cafés or restaurants.

Naturally, there are many jobs in Aotearoa which don't follow the nine-to-five system. Careers in the police, hospitals, prisons, dairy factories, and the like involve shift work, while workers involved in seasonal labor, such as farmers and orchardists, will work long hours in summer and shorter ones in winter.

SHOPS AND BANKS

Stores and malls in New Zealand usually open at 9:00 a.m. and close between 5:00 and 5:30 p.m., Monday to Saturday. Supermarkets are open every day from 7:00 or 8:00 a.m., but closing hours vary. "Dairies" (convenience stores) also have extended hours and sell a range of groceries, candy, ice cream, and takeaway food.

Bank branches are usually open from 9:00 a.m. to 4:30 p.m., Monday to Friday and are closed on the weekend.

Most shop purchases are made using bank cards and mobile payment apps. Cash is still widely accepted and ATMs are easy enough to find, just make sure your card is PIN-ready before arriving in order to withdraw cash and make payments in store. As of 2021, cheques are no longer in use in New Zealand.

Overall, New Zealand doesn't have a culture of bargaining; what you see is usually what you get. As such, prices are not negotiable in small to medium shops, market stalls, or supermarkets. However, some national retailers have a policy of matching or beating competitors' prices. Many will also give discounts on electronics and appliances if you ask, particularly if you're buying several products—you have nothing to lose by asking!

All goods and services are subject to a 15 percent Goods and Services Tax called GST which is included in the displayed price of an item.

TELEVISION AND OTHER MEDIA

Radio broadcasting in New Zealand began in 1922, followed by television which started in 1960 and color TV arriving in the 1970s. That decade also saw rapid growth in the production of local content, including popular drama series and soap operas. Broadcasting was deregulated in the 1980s and the switch to digital television in 2013 provided another big boost for the industry.

Today, digital television and radio are available throughout New Zealand via the Freeview digital platform. Netflix and other streaming channels are now standard in many New Zealand homes. However, cell phone coverage can be patchy in many rural areas, while broadband is non-existent. Sky and Freeview are the television lifelines for these communities.

There are many private and local radio stations, including twenty-one Maori stations and a national Maori-language news service. At the same time, Pacific

Island and other immigrant and community groups have started their own radio and television services. The government retains the National Radio, Concert FM, Radio New Zealand external services, and the parliamentary broadcasting service.

TV and radio programs are listed daily in the newspapers and on the Internet. Some stations exclusively broadcast talk shows. Tuning in to them gives visitors an idea of the polarizing issues that concern some Kiwis. Be warned, they also offer a chance for callers to show their bias; strong opinions make for interesting shows.

Older Kiwis still read a lot, but there is a worrying decline in reading for pleasure among younger age groups. New Zealand adults read books, newspapers, and magazines for pleasure and information, enjoying both physical and digital formats. Second-hand book fairs are alive and well, with people flocking to sift through the enormous piles of donated books as they search for a bargain.

KIWIANA

New Zealand's popular culture incorporates elements from the heritage of its many residents. You can find it in food, clothing, toys, emblems, and even dances that are uniquely Kiwi. Collectively they're called "Kiwiana" because they show what New Zealanders have used and enjoyed over the years. Most Kiwiana are still used

Freshly baked Anzac biscuits, made with rolled oats and golden syrup.

in New Zealand today and form part of the culture's collective identity. Kiwis who live overseas often pine for a taste of home when they think of these things.

There is much rivalry between New Zealand and Australia over some favorite Kiwi icons. Each country claims to be the inventor of the Pavlova dessert, and many New Zealanders are still annoyed that Australia claims Phar Lap, an acclaimed New Zealand-bred racehorse, as its own.

Kiwiana includes:
- **The Haka** A Maori ceremonial war dance
- **Buzzy Bee** A child's toy in colors of red and yellow
- **No. 8 Wire** An all-purpose wire, symbol of Kiwi ingenuity and adaptability
- **Paua Shell** For jewelry and ornaments
- **Jandals** Thonged sandals, or flip-flops
- **Gumboots** Originally made of black rubber, gumboots now come in many colors and waterproof materials.

A paua shell and silver wire necklace pendant.

- **Pavlova** A dessert of fruit and cream on a generous meringue base
- **Fish and Chips**
- **Meat Pies**
- **Vogel's Bread** A full grain bread
- **Hokey Pokey** Ice cream
- **L&P** A drink made from lemon and carbonated water from the town of Paeroa
- **Anzac Biscuits** Rolled oats and golden syrup cookies
- **Vegemite** A yeast spread, based on the UK's Marmite
- **Bluff Oysters** The best oysters in the country, caught off the southern coast
- **Lamingtons** Sponge cakes covered with chocolate icing and rolled in desiccated coconut
- **Pineapple Lumps** Chewy, chocolate-coated pineapple-flavored candy.

CHAPTER SIX

TIME OUT

Wherever you go in Aotearoa, almost every gathering includes a meal of some kind, whether at a "barbie," a gala fundraising dinner, or a shared meal at home.

New Zealand's cuisine has moved far from its early British roots. Nowadays, food and cooking styles are enriched by immigrants from all over the world and traditional Maori ingredients feature in restaurants and home kitchens. The New Zealand climate grows many vegetables, including aubergines (eggplant), zucchini, and *kumara* (sweet potato), as well as carrots, peas, leafy greens, and cauliflower. Visit any of the multicultural markets to see the diversity; all sorts of fresh and inexpensive produce can be bought and even tasted beforehand. Otara Market in South Auckland and the Sunday market at Avondale to the west of the city are well worth visiting.

Stone and pip fruit grow particularly well, too. Citrus fruit needs the warmer climate of the North Island, while the South Island grows apricots, peaches, plums, nectarines, and cherries. Kiwifruit is grown commercially from Tauranga to Gisborne, while berries, apples, and pears grow everywhere.

EATING OUT

There is no shortage of international cuisine in New Zealand, from Japanese, Vietnamese, Thai, and Indian to European, South American, and Pacific. Most restaurants are "*á la carte*," where you order from a set menu. A few have extensive buffets where you can serve yourself from a choice of dishes set out on tables. New Zealand's restaurants compare favorably with those

Enjoy views of Queenstown and Lake Wakatipu at the Skyline Café, perched 1500 feet (450 meters) above ground on Bob's Peak.

overseas, but even upscale restaurants tend to have quite a casual feel.

Dress for dining out is informal, too. Restaurants expect a tidy appearance, but few require suits and ties. Smoking is banned in bars and restaurants, though many provide a covered outdoor area for smokers to use.

Food is not particularly cheap in New Zealand, and that's reflected in restaurant prices. While you're likely to find some reasonably priced lunch menus, it is not economical to eat out every night.

"Bring Your Own"

Some restaurants are BYO, or "bring your own bottle," and display this in their window and advertisements. However, they will charge corkage and as prices vary considerably, it is sensible to check the cost in advance.

Unless you're at a vegetarian restaurant, you will find meat, fish, and chicken on the menu, usually accompanied by vegetables or salad. Grass-fed New Zealand lamb is internationally recognized for its lean, tender qualities. You're most likely to find it roasted, as chops, or as tender lamb shanks in Kiwi restaurants. New Zealand beef is also outstanding, and you'll find at least one cut of steak in most restaurants. Many restaurants also offer pork and venison as red meat options.

Unsurprisingly, given its location, New Zealand has a thriving fishing industry and *kaimoana*, seafood, comes in many forms. There are white-fleshed fish such as "snapper" (a North Island fish) and "blue cod" (from the South Island). Fresh or saltwater salmon, tuna, oysters, and green-lipped mussels are all likely to be on the menu, especially in coastal cities and towns.

New Zealand is one of only four places globally where you'll find *inanga* whitebait (the others being Chile, Argentina, and the southern Australian coastline.) It is worth trying these tiny seasonal fish that spawn in a small number of bays off the South Island. They are caught from early September to mid-November and usually appear on restaurant and cafe menus as "whitebait fritters." Saltwater crayfish or spiny rock lobsters are also a popular but expensive item, so it's no wonder that recreational fishers like to catch them when they can.

TIPPING

Service charges and tips are not included in receipts, and tipping is not a traditional New Zealand practice. However, it is becoming more common, especially in higher-end establishments, and 10 percent of the check is acceptable. Also, expect to pay an additional service charge on statutory holidays to cover the increase in staffing costs.

Bluff oysters are considered a great delicacy, but they're not available year-round. They live wild in the chilly waters of Foveaux Strait near Stewart Island and are harvested from March until June or July. Southlanders are so keen on the oysters' exquisite flavor that they celebrate the season at the Bluff Oyster Festival in May.

Table Manners

Table manners follow European customs, including holding your knife in the right hand and a fork in the left. When you've finished eating, place the knife and fork, tines pointing up and the knife parallel, in the middle of the plate. Even if you still have food on the plate, the waiter will understand that you've had enough.

Trying Maori Fare

For those interested in trying Maori fare, it can often be found served at Maori concert evenings, especially in the Rotorua area. Most visitors enjoy a *hangi,* where food is cooked in an earth oven—a hole in the ground is lined with hot rocks and the resulting steam cooks the food. Baskets of foil-wrapped meat, fish, vegetables, and shellfish are covered with cabbage leaves, and soil is heaped on top. Cooking takes several hours, and it's a delicate art to get the timing right. Maori in the Rotorua district traditionally cooked food in the many thermal hot pools, but that is rarely possible in modern times.

Puha is a well-known food akin to watercress. Maori boil this up with pork bones and potatoes, making for a hearty winter dish, especially when accompanied by *rewena*, a potato sourdough bread.

Another traditional food source is the sooty shearwater, known locally as the muttonbird (*titi*). The colloquial name came from the early European settlers, who preserved the duck-like bird in salt and thought its oily flesh tasted like preserved mutton. Only a few Maori families have the right to gather *titi* from the remote Titi Islands off the southern coast each year. Then, after the harvest, muttonbirds are sometimes available alongside fresh fish in the larger supermarkets.

Takeaways

New Zealanders love take-out food. Fish and chips are the number one choice, with savory pies coming a close second, but there are many other options. You'll find burger giants like McDonald's and Burger King, but every small-town fish and chip store also sells a variety of burgers, from beef to vegetarian. Pizza is another favorite, as are Indian, Chinese, and Thai takeaways. Sushi bars are trendy, and you will find one in most towns. Many outlets offer delivery services in urban areas. Food delivery services such as Uber Eats and Delivereasy also operate in many cities around the country.

Café Culture

Kiwis adore coffee, and the country has a thriving café culture, with more coffee roasters per capita than anywhere in the world. People meet each other for coffee at the drop of a hat, although town coffee bars differ from rural ones and offer more choice. Coffee carts are a popular small business and appear at most events and gatherings. Some carts have a route around the camping grounds in summer, where people rush to grab a cup of their favorite morning brew.

You are spoiled for choice by the wide variety of coffee drinks available, too.

FLAT WHITE

New Zealand has gained the distinction among the world's coffee aficionados as pioneering the "flat white," which, according to Kiwi baristas, is a less milky brew with textured rather than frothy milk, and often served with two shots of coffee. On the spectrum of coffee varieties, it is stronger than a latte, but smoother than a cappuccino.

FARMERS' MARKETS

In every town, weekend farmers' markets sell seasonal produce. The Napier and Hastings markets are a typical example. There are strawberries and asparagus in spring, veggies, berries, and stone fruit in summer. In fall (autumn), you'll find avocados and olive oil, with citrus fruit in winter. One fruit that does particularly well in the Bay of Plenty is the feijoa (pineapple guava), which has a distinctive aroma. It can be eaten raw, on its own, added to fruit salad, or peeled and baked with native Manuka honey. It also makes delicious jam and chutney. Tamarillos, or tree tomatoes, originally from South America, are another popular winter fruit.

Herbs are plentiful, and often grown organically. Maori herbs include *pikopiko,* a fern frond similar to the European and American fiddlehead fern. *Horopito*, with its peppery leaves, is tasty on grilled fish and is also an ingredient in salad dressings.

New Zealand's cheese industry is booming, and consumers are spoiled for choice. Award-winning food producer Kapiti is renowned for its different varieties of cheese and continues to be one of New Zealand's top specialty cheesemakers. Try the creamy Kikorangi, soft white Kotuku and Camembert, Pakari aged and smoked cheddar, and Kapiti Brick, a washed-rind variety.

Local honey is another high-quality product that you can find at most markets. Kiwis traditionally eat clover honey, but Manuka honey is the most valuable and widely exported crop because of its healing properties.

Over two thousand specialty food manufacturers produce everyday and gourmet products for the local and international markets. In keeping with the clean, green image of New Zealand, many smaller food producers are certified, organic growers. Products like quinoa, hemp, and saffron are becoming popular, and there is a growing selection of gluten-free food.

ALCOHOL

Alcohol is a normal part of Kiwi social life, with beer and wine being the most popular drinks. That said, it is always socially acceptable to ask for a non-alcoholic drink and is a good idea if you will be driving afterwards—drink-driving in Aotearoa is heavily penalized.

There are liquor stores in many cities and towns, and beer and wine are available at most supermarkets. The legal drinking age in New Zealand is eighteen years, and the onus is on retailers to establish your age before you can purchase any alcohol. They face huge fines if they're caught selling to under-eighteens, so most will ask for ID just to make sure.

Be aware that some city centers and beachfronts have liquor ban areas, particularly in resort areas over the summer vacation season. You cannot consume or even carry alcohol in these areas. The police may ask you to empty bottles and can arrest you if you don't.

Beer

According to a 2019 report by the New Zealand Institute for Economic Research, New Zealand has 218 breweries, which is more per capita than the United Kingdom, Australia, and the United States. As well as the well-established Speights and Dominion Breweries, there are a wealth of boutique breweries producing craft beer, which is becoming ever more popular. Most of these have taprooms where you can try the beers on site.

Aotearoa also has a sizable hop-growing industry, with 85 percent of the annual harvest heading overseas.

Wine

New Zealand winemaking has surged in recent years and is now a billion-dollar export industry. The country has some 2,023 vineyards, from Northland to Central Otago, with Sauvignon Blanc being the most significant variety making up 63 percent of grape varieties grown. In the last few years, NZ Pinot Noir has become a best-seller abroad; the cool nights, bright sunshine, and high UV levels in central Otago make it the ideal spot for growing this fussy grape. New Zealand's wineries range from large, established companies to tiny boutique vineyards. Most offer tours and wine tasting. Others have restaurants attached and are a popular venue for weddings and gatherings.

To find great local drinks, head to a beer festival or follow a "wine trail" which will take you to some of the best wineries in each area. Sometimes you can go on bus tours, which take you around the popular spots or to tiny, out-of-the-way establishments.

SHOPPING FOR LEISURE

Kiwis often love to hang out in shopping malls, where they can browse and buy or relax over a coffee. The enclosed malls usually include at least one supermarket, many national chain stores, and a few smaller, individual

Shoppers and diners enjoying Queenstown's Arts and Crafts Market, held every Saturday in Earnslaw Park.

brands. There is almost always a food court, with stalls selling ethnic food and usually a burger outlet. Spread out around the main corridors, you'll also find other food stalls selling coffee, muffins, and healthier options like smoothies and salads.

At the other end of the scale, "op-shops" selling second-hand clothes, toys, bric-a-brac, and furniture are rising in popularity. As economic realities bite, many Kiwis are spending less, while environmental considerations means more and more are happy to buy preloved goods rather than new. Others simply enjoy browsing around, hoping to find a bargain.

The Govett-Brewster Art Gallery in New Plymouth, North Island.

CULTURE

Music, literature, art, and crafts all play important roles in New Zealand's cultural life. There's a national opera company, ballet company, and symphony orchestra, as well as smaller, regional ones. There are art galleries and theaters galore, awards for artistic achievement and grants for new talent. *Kapa haka* groups perform traditional and modern Maori songs and dances, while other groups keep Pacific art, music, and dance strong in New Zealand; art in New Zealand is diverse.

The Dunedin Art Gallery, on the South Island, is the oldest in Aotearoa, while the Christchurch Arts Centre features galleries, museums, cinemas, boutique retailers, artisan eateries and bars, and holds a variety of events under its historic roof. Many smaller towns hold annual art festivals where local and national artists are encouraged to exhibit. Others have museums, ranging from quaint to modern, featuring their local history and culture. In Hawera, the privately owned Tawhiti Museum has an extensive series of large and small dioramas—all handmade by the owner—giving a fascinating glimpse into the history of the Taranaki region. Down south, the tiny town of Waikaia recently upgraded the Switzers Museum, which showcases the area's rich gold mining history. At the other end of the country, Whangarei is home to the brand-new Hundertwasser Art Centre, the opening for which was delayed from 2020 owing to the coronavirus pandemic. Initially designed in 1993, this building will be the newest and last authentic Hundertwasser building in the world.

The national museum of Aotearoa, Te Papa, is in Wellington. Sitting on a major fault line, the building is supported by 152 base isolators—shock absorbers made of rubber and lead—which protect it from earthquakes and allow it to sway safely one meter in any direction. The museum preserves New Zealand's important cultural heritage and hosts a wealth of permanent and temporary exhibits. One of the most striking of these is the Gallipoli exhibition. Commemorating Anzac history from 1915–16, it features eight larger-than-life scenes, showing the stories of real New Zealanders during the campaign. Another popular exhibit is the carefully preserved colossal squid, the largest specimen of its kind ever caught. Weighing around 1030 lbs (470 kgs), the squid had become entangled in fishing nets off Antarctica's coast and died before it could be released.

Music and Dance

There are vibrant and energetic music and dance scenes in New Zealand, but to make a living many New Zealanders have taken their talent overseas. Kiri Te Kanawa is probably the best-known of New Zealand's many international opera singers, while country music fans have probably heard of Keith Urban—also a Kiwi. Rock legend Neil Finn was an integral part of Split Enz and Crowded House before joining Fleetwood Mac in 2018. Lorde's first hit single "Royals" won two Grammys in 2014, and at the other end of the spectrum comic duo Flight of the Conchords endeared worldwide audiences with their eccentric Kiwi humor.

Cabaret singer-dancer Mika Haka, with his dance company Torotoro, performs worldwide. Choreographer and dancer Parris Goebel has worked her magic with A-listers like Justin Bieber and Jennifer Lopez.

Writing

Storytelling is central to Maori culture and many of their songs are also poems. One noted collection of these is *Nga Moteatea*, compiled by Sir Apirana Ngata. Poets include Hone Tuwhare, Fleur Adcock, Bill Manhire, and Brian Turner, while Katherine Mansfield is world-renowned for her short stories. In downtown Wellington, her hometown, there is a stately statue of Katherine wearing an intricate dress made of words from her most famous stories.

New Zealand novelists write for adults and children in all genres. Man-Booker Prize winners include

Keri Hulme for *The Bone People* in 1985; Lloyd Jones for *Mister Pip* in 2007; and Eleanor Catton with *The Luminaries* in 2013, a thrilling evocation of the shenanigans on the New Zealand goldfields in the nineteenth century. Children's author Margaret Mahy was so beloved in New Zealand that Christchurch city built an innovative inner-city playground in her honor.

Movies

Kiwis love watching movies and there is a thriving homegrown movie scene too. Movies in the '90s such as Jane Campion's *The Piano*, Lee Tamahori's *Once Were Warriors*, and *Whale Rider* did much to showcase local talent and put New Zealand's film-makers on the map. Later, in the early 2000s, Sir Peter Jackson's *Lord of the Rings* trilogy threw New Zealand's other-worldly landscapes into the limelight; the final film in the trilogy, *The Return of the King*, grossed US $1 billion at the box office and won Oscars in all the eleven categories for which it was nominated.

Since then, Hollywood producers have flocked to New Zealand. *Avatar 2* and *3, Chronicles of Narnia,* and Disney's *Mulan* are just some of the many movies that have since been set in the country, and there is now industry-wide recognition of the professional film crews and studio facilities on offer. New Zealand is also home to Weta Workshops. This Wellington studio is at the forefront of digital special effects and props. You can take a tour of their operation and see the magic behind *Middle Earth, Superman, The Adventures of Tintin,* and more.

SPORTS

Sports are a vital part of life on Aotearoa; from athletics to zorb ball, fun runs to Ironman triathlons, they play an important role in recreation on this temperate island. On any given day, you'll find Kiwis in or on the water, hang gliding off cliffs or parachuting out of planes. They'll be hunting in the backcountry and tramping in the mountains or bush, swinging a tennis racket, or smashing a squash ball.

It helps that sports are well funded by the government, which has provided millions in funding for high schools and local groups, as well as athletes who show potential. Many Kiwis of all ages are involved with sports clubs or join in less organized activities like boating or biking on one of the many cycle trails.

Kiwis are keen spectators too, and often get together to watch a big match on TV; you may well find yourself invited, especially if you are from the same country as the opposing team! There'll be plenty of good-natured teasing and Kiwis will like it if you can contribute. Indeed, discussing sports, be it in a social or a business environment, is often a good icebreaker, especially if you show interest in New Zealand's national or regional teams.

Major Sports

There's no denying that Kiwis love their rugby and for all intents and purposes it is the national sport. Both the All Blacks and the Black Ferns (the men and women's national teams) perform at the top of the world stage, and both have won multiple World Cups. New Zealanders have incredibly high expectations of their national teams and are not pleased when they lose—particularly if it is to Australia.

Maori and Pacific Islanders are a vital part of New Zealand rugby and make up a considerable proportion of the national, sevens, and rugby league teams.

There are many variations of rugby that attract players of all ages and abilities. Touch rugby is a popular social game of running and passing. Many businesses and social clubs field mixed teams of men and women over the summer months. "Sevens" rugby is a fast-moving game with a circuit of international tournaments as well as provincial and club matches. Rugby League, which has slightly different rules to "regular" rugby, is also popular.

The national All Blacks Sevens team in action against Fiji.

The national league team is called The Kiwis, and the country fields one team—The Warriors—in the competitive Australian league.

FAIR PLAY!

No account of rugby in New Zealand would be complete without mention of the 1981 tour of South Africa's national team, the Springboks. It divided the country and is still hotly contested today. Most Kiwis disapproved of South Africa's policies on apartheid at the time, but the prime minister, Robert Muldoon, refused to stop the tour, on the basis that politics had no place in sports. The situation was responsible for days of protests, police intervention, and arrests. But the event provoked an opportunity to address the issue of racism in New Zealand.

Rugby may be the national game, but even more people play soccer, especially at a recreational level. Perhaps that's not surprising given the number of immigrants who hail from countries where football is the "beautiful game." Again, NZ soccer has one team—The Phoenix—which plays in the Aussie football league. Futsal, a fast-paced indoor version of football, is also growing in popularity.

Netball is the sport most favored by women in New Zealand, though today it is played by both men and women country-wide. There is a fiercely fought national competition, and the national team, the Silver Ferns, are currently at the top of the international tables. Only the Australian Diamonds regularly beat them and, as you can by now imagine, matches between the two teams cause massive public excitement. The men's national netball team is also fiercely athletic and provides valuable competition for the Silver Ferns whenever the two teams meet.

Cricket is a popular summer sport with both children and adults. The Black Caps men's national team is currently top or near top of the world rankings in all three forms (twenty20, one-day, and test formats). When cricket-lovers aren't flocking to the ovals to play or watch, they play "backyard cricket"; all that's needed is an open space, a ball and bat, and a set of rudimentary stumps of some kind. Many international players learned their first cricket skills by batting and bowling against their dads, cousins, and friends in the backyard. The game is so popular that the Black Caps even offered to play a backyard cricket game as a prize in one nationwide competition.

Other Sports and Activities

More than a quarter of Kiwis enjoy watching and playing golf. It is not as elitist a sport in New Zealand as it is in some countries, and most club membership and green fees are very affordable. There are more than four hundred golf courses around the country, one of the highest per capita in the world. They range from professionally designed courses like Millbrook and The Hills in Arrowtown (which regularly host the New Zealand Golf Open) down to nine-hole rural clubs with ten-dollar green fees.

Field hockey is popular with both men and women, and basketball has a big following among teenagers and those in their twenties. Skiing and snowboarding are favorite winter pastimes. There are fifteen ski fields throughout the Southern Alps. Australians flock to Queenstown each year for its excellent slopes, while Aucklanders and Wellingtonians take weekends away on Ruapehu's two North Island fields.

Extreme sports are popular too, possibly started by bungee jumping, a New Zealand invention which is now enjoyed by thrill seekers worldwide.

Another locally invented sport is jet boating. Sir William Hamilton created the waterjet engine in 1954 for use in New Zealand's fast-flowing, shallow rivers, and Kiwis have been jet boating ever since. In fact, rafting, canoeing, kayaking—and probably any other water sport you can name—all abound in the pools, rivers, lakes, and oceans of Aotearoa.

Boating and Recreational Fishing

New Zealand is surrounded by water so it is not surprising that boats feature heavily in recreational life. There are many beautiful harbors and bays for boating of all kinds, including Northland's Bay of Islands,

Jet boating: not for the fainthearted or those who have recently had lunch.

Auckland's Waitemata Harbour, and the beautiful bays and inlets of Lyttelton Harbour, near Christchurch. Kiwis also spend a lot of time boating and water skiing on lakes around New Zealand. A favorite holiday involves parking the caravan by a lake and taking the boat out.

In Aotearoa, fishing is a popular pastime; some fish for food and others for the sport and thrill of landing a wily trout or marlin. Huge fish are often mounted as trophies while others are released back into the river or ocean.

You'll find anglers of all ages dangling a hand line off piers and bridges or trying to catch salmon or trout in freshwater lakes and rivers. Fly-fishing here is recognized as being among the world's best. This casting method is used in both North Island and South Island rivers. It's mandatory on some trout river sections, which also have a strict daily catch limit.

Some people go surfcasting off the shores and rocks for snapper, *terakihi* (a morwong species), or *kahawai* (what the Aussies call Australian Salmon). Others go out onto the ocean for blue cod and crayfish, especially in Southland and the West Coast. In Northland, there is big game fishing for tuna and marlin in the Pacific Ocean.

Kaimoana, "food from the sea," plays a prominent role in Maori culture. Mussels are gathered, as are *pipi* (a type of small mollusk), and *paua* (sea snails, also known as New Zealand abalone or perlemoen). *Paua* are highly prized for their meat but also for their

Fly fishing near Lake Taupo, North Island.

beautiful inner shell; with its iridescent greens and blues, it is used in carvings, jewelry, and souvenirs.

Snorkelers and divers go spearfishing off the coast. Others swim in the marine reserves of Northland, Kapiti, Nelson, and others, to admire but not catch the diverse sea life that flourishes in those protected waters. Altogether, Aotearoa has forty-four marine reserves spread around the mainland coast and outer islands.

New Zealand has seven fishing areas, and you need to know the specific rules and regulations for the place that you're fishing. As the rules can change, it pays to check before you embark on a trip in order to avoid any issues.

FESTIVALS AND EVENTS

New Zealand has a wide variety of annual festivals, sporting events, concerts, and shows ranging from music and culture to wine and food, as well as seasonal celebrations. The following is a sample of what is on offer (ask at information centers for a list of local events, shows, and festivals):

January: Wellington Summer City. A month-long festival program held throughout the city
January: Christchurch Buskers Festival
February: Marlborough Wine Festival
February: Art Deco Weekend, Napier

March: Golden Shears Sheep-shearing contest, Masterton

March: Pasifika Festival. Auckland celebrates the music, food, arts, and dance of the Pacific Island communities

March (every two years): Te Matatini National Kapa Haka Festival is the premier indigenous cultural event in New Zealand and the world's largest celebration of Maori traditional performing arts

March: WOMAD (World of Music, Arts and Dance) in New Plymouth

March: Hokitika Wildfoods Festival

March/April (every two years): Warbirds Over Wanaka international air show

May: Bluff Oyster and Food Festival in Southland

May–June: Tussock Country Music Festival in Gore, Southland

May–June (every three years): The Ocean Race. Yachts race across the world's oceans, and Auckland is one of the stopovers

June: Fieldays Mystery Creek. An agricultural show in Waikato

September–October: World of Wearable Arts, Wellington

October: PIC Coastal Classic. A yacht race from Auckland to Russell, the biggest coastal race in New Zealand

November: Canterbury Show Week, Christchurch Agricultural in flavor, with family entertainment

November: Hunter's Garden, Marlborough. New Zealand's premier gardening event

December: Rhythm and Vines. A popular music and

camping festival held near Gisborne from the December 28 to January 1 to celebrate the New Year. Wanaka holds a sister event called Rhythm & Alps.

TAKING A BREAK

Kiwis like to take vacations, so if you are visiting New Zealand at peak times, such as Christmas and Easter, then plan far ahead as accommodation often gets booked up early. You also need to take note of Kiwi holidays, such as the Queen's birthday weekend, Labour Day, Waitangi, and Anzac Day, as many people take the opportunity to turn these into long weekends if possible. Booking ahead with domestic flights and rental vehicles is also recommended for these periods.

As the winter can be wet, gray, and miserable, many New Zealanders take off to Australia's warmer east coast. Queensland's Gold Coast, south of Brisbane, is a favorite, as is the Sunshine Coast, with Noosa probably being the most popular destination. There are plenty of package vacations on offer, which include flights, accommodation, and meals.

Other favorite Kiwi destinations include the many tropical Pacific Islands, such as Fiji, Rarotonga in the Cook Islands, Aitutaki, and, further away, Tahiti, Vanuatu, Samoa, and Tonga.

CHAPTER SEVEN

TRAVEL, HEALTH, & SAFETY

ARRIVING AND DEPARTING

Every person entering New Zealand must be in possession of a valid passport that does not expire for at least one month after their planned departure date. Around sixty countries are on New Zealand's visa free list, which allows their passport holders to vacation for up to three months without a visitor visa. You will need to apply for a visitor's visa if your country is not on the list. If you are traveling to New Zealand for business purposes you will need a Business Visitor Visa.

People intending to stay more than twelve months need to submit a General Medical Certificate too and residents of some countries will also need to submit a certificate proving that they are free from tuberculosis. In 2020 New Zealand closed its borders to all but New Zealand citizens, residents, and essential workers. This restriction remained in place in 2021 at the time of writing. When the borders do reopen, there are likely to be new rules around Covid-19 including tests and proof of vaccination. Visit www.immigration.govt.nz for official information on New Zealand's latest visa and entry requirements.

There is currently no entry tax, but a departure tax is included in your airfare. There is a lot of debate around this, and a "tourist entry tax" may be implemented in future.

New Zealand is dependent on agriculture and as such takes its biosecurity seriously. It is forbidden to bring any plants or plant products into the country, including herbal medicines and fruit. You can't bring in any food, animal products, or products from endangered species either and you are required to declare artifacts such as wooden carvings, dirty sports gear, or items that have been in contact with the soil. Customs officers may sterilize or fumigate these before allowing them in. If you have medication be ready to show your prescription. However, cannabis and other controlled drugs are illegal; you'll be fined, jailed, or deported if you're caught with them. It is also illegal to bring weapons and objectionable publications into New Zealand.

Signs all over the airport very clearly state the rules, and there are amnesty bins to dump items in before reaching customs. Should you have anything that is vacuum-packed, declare it. Declare anything if in doubt. There will usually be sniffer dogs checking the baggage. Visit www.customs.govt.nz and www.quarantine.govt.nz for the most up-to-date information on this topic.

Some items can't be taken out of the country, including wildlife or objects on the International Trade in Endangered Species list. Maori artifacts over fifty years old, bones, feathers, or other parts of extinct New Zealand species cannot leave the country. Nor may you take any goods over fifty years old that have national, scientific, or artistic significance.

WHEN TO VISIT AND WHAT TO DO

You can visit New Zealand all year round, because the climate is temperate and the attractions are so varied. November through April are the warmer months and the most popular, though storms and cold fronts can still occur and so you should come prepared. February and March usually have the warmest and most settled weather. If you want a skiing holiday, then mid-June through September is your best bet. Bear in mind that Christmas and New Year coincide with the long school vacation so accommodation and flights will be harder to find in December and January. It's best to book well in advance. Even though it's officially mid-summer, January weather can be very unsettled. Northland, Marlborough, the West Coast, and Southland can have rainstorms and floods. In February and March, the "gray brigade" (retirees, that is) often hit the road in their campers and caravans.

There is plenty to do throughout the year but as mentioned, it is a good idea to book ahead if you are visiting during peak times. Year-round activities include bungee jumping, cycling, and wine and beer tasting. Why not try whale watching, kiwi and wildlife spotting, or exploring caves. See www.newzealand.com for more ideas.

New Zealand offers excellent and varied winter skiing and boarding on ski fields of all sizes. In summer, there are boat trips, sea and river kayaking, rafting, and jet boating adventures. You can swim with dolphins, go canyoning, tramping, or simply enjoy time at the beach, to name a few.

When packing clothes, bring things that you can put on or peel off, such as T-shirts, sweaters, and jackets. Don't forget rainwear; you're sure to need it on your trip.

GETTING AROUND

New Zealand is not a large country, especially compared to its Tasman neighbor, and travel is relatively easy and efficient. You'll find several public transport options, although nothing to compare with the extensive subway systems of cities like London, Tokyo, or New York. Kiwis themselves prefer cars or motorbikes.

CITY TRANSPORT

Some New Zealand cities sprawl across many miles; others are relatively compact, making it easier to get around. Buses are the primary public transport in all cities and large towns and run frequently on weekdays during the peak travel times. Otherwise, they run hourly or half-hourly. Although you can pay for fares using cash, most companies encourage commuters to use a travel card. Because different companies run the city buses, commuter cards differ from city to city. Aucklanders use an ATHop card, Wellingtonians have Snapper, while in Christchurch, it's called a Metro Card. All these cards are prepaid. If you stay a while in one city and intend to travel by bus, it will be cheaper and more convenient to buy a travel card than to pay cash as you go.

Only Auckland and Wellington have commuter train services. In Auckland, train lines extend from the central terminal of Britomart to some central, southern, and western suburbs. Wellington's train service has been running longer and connects downtown Wellington with the wider region.

Both cities also run ferries across their harbors and there's also a short ferry service around Lyttelton harbor near Christchurch. Auckland commuter ferries run between downtown Auckland and Devonport on the North Shore, East Auckland, and Waiheke Island. Again, you can pay cash fares or use your ATHop card (which also works for train journeys).

Wellington's ferry service goes from downtown Queens Wharf to Seatoun, Matiu/Somes Island, and Days Bay. You can buy one-way or return tickets or purchase concession cards either at Queens Wharf or on board the ferry.

Most cities and large towns in New Zealand have taxi services. There are also various ride-share options, especially in Auckland, Wellington, and Christchurch. Uber operates in 13 cities and towns, including Queenstown, Hamilton, and Tauranga, while Ola and Zoomy are only available in the three main centers. Taxis tend to be expensive, and ride-shares usually a little cheaper.

Bicycles, electric scooters, and walking are the other options for traveling in a city or town. Currently, Auckland, Christchurch, Hamilton, Wellington, and Dunedin have dock-free electric scooter options run by Lime, Flamingo, or Neuron. Other towns are trialing various hire systems and brands.

There are plenty of little businesses that hire bikes or scooters for anything from half an hour to several weeks. Many cities have—or are building—a network

of cycle paths so that cyclists can avoid riding on busy roads. You'll also find marked cycle lanes on some city roads. In general, bicycles should not be ridden on sidewalks. It is permitted, however, on some shared walkways which can be identified by signs and painted arrows indicating direction. Scooters are slightly different—some places permit riders to use them on the sidewalk, others say to stay on the road. Wherever and whatever you ride, be aware of other road and path users. It is compulsory to wear a helmet when cycling on the road, path, or cycleway. In 2021 it was not mandatory to wear a helmet on a scooter, but it is highly recommended, and the law may change in future. It's best to check before you ride.

INTERCITY TRANSPORT

Flying

Air travel is the fastest way to travel long distances. Most international planes enter New Zealand through the Auckland or Christchurch international airports, then transfer you to a domestic airline. Air New Zealand, the national airline, services a network of domestic airports on both main islands. Smaller operators offer flights to Stewart Island, Great Barrier Island, and the Chatham Islands.

Until 2020, Jetstar and Qantas also had flights between Auckland, Wellington, Christchurch, and Queenstown. These flights were often cheaper than Air NZ flights, but during the pandemic, Qantas pulled out altogether, and Jetstar ran a limited system which only operated when the country was in the lowest alert level, Level One.

Air New Zealand's standard seats can be expensive, but they frequently offer sales and budget options if you book your flights well ahead. Most airlines provide electronic booking options, and it's usually more convenient to book on the Internet. However, there are travel agents in all cities if you prefer to book over the counter, and you can buy last-minute tickets at the airport. In 2021, it was mandatory to wear face masks on all passenger flights. Whether that continues into future years remains to be seen.

Buses

There is an extensive bus network over each island. Intercity operates New Zealand's largest passenger transport network and there are local companies specific to various areas. Services between the main cities usually operate several times a day and throughout the week.

There are also shuttle services, operated by smaller companies, and some geared especially to overseas visitors and backpackers. These are a good alternative for traveling into the city from airports. One such company, Kiwi Experience, offers all-in-one package tours which allow you to get on and off where you please.

Buses are reliable and comfortable, and usually run on time, but there can be congestion on weekends, especially when leaving major centers on a Friday afternoon and arriving back on Sunday evening. Travel can be much slower on long weekends and peak seasonal times.

North of Auckland, there is one major road out of the city, State Highway One, which begins at the Northern Motorway. Eventually, it forks to follow the west coast via Dargaville or goes straight on to Paihia and the Bay of Islands. There are also alternative winding coastal roads that aren't on the bus routes. South of Auckland, the highways fan out, with State Highway 1 running through the center. SH2 goes down the east coast, and SH3 goes to the west. Other state highways and local roads connect these major routes, winding around and over the mountain ranges to end in Wellington.

On the South Island, SH1 continues down the east coast to Bluff in Southland. State Highway 6 travels along the west coast, and two routes track down the center. There are three main passes between the east and west coasts: Arthurs Pass, Lewis Pass, and the more southerly Haast Pass. Coaches travel between towns on these and many other state highways every day.

Trains

Once, New Zealand had an extensive railway network, but in the 1950s, cars became commonplace, and one by one, the rail routes closed. The remaining lines are primarily used for freight, but three long-distance passenger trains operate several times a week and offer spectacular views. The Coastal Pacific from Christchurch to Picton runs along the South Island's

Scenery on the TranzAlpine Express from Christchurch to Greymount.

rugged northeast coast while the TranzAlpine train passes through the magnificent mountain scenery of the Southern Alps on its way from Christchurch to Greymouth. You can travel to a range of destinations on the line between Auckland and Wellington on the Northern Explorer in the North Island. There is also a shorter service called the Capital Connection, from Palmerston North to Wellington.

Ferries

Two ferry companies cross Cook Strait: Blue Bridge and the Interislander. Both will cancel services in rough seas. Car ferries also operate between Auckland and Waiheke and out to Great Barrier Island in the Hauraki Gulf. There's a passenger-only ferry between Bluff and Stewart Island and small car ferries on the Hokianga Harbor and the Bay of Islands in Northland. Check online for up-to-date schedules.

Marlborough Sounds, Picton, South Island.

Car Rental

Driving a car is the most flexible way to see Aotearoa. Although the main highways are quick and efficient, time permitting, the alternative Scenic Routes are highly recommended. There are six such routes on the North Island, all of which are signposted and carry enticing names like "Surf Highway 45," "The Volcanic Loop," and "Forgotten World." The scenery can be breathtaking. The South Island has three official Scenic Routes. Inland Route 72 showcases South Canterbury and takes you past some of its biggest ski fields, the Alpine Pacific Triangle is a loop around North Canterbury, taking you from the Pacific Ocean to the mountains and back through vineyards, though the most spectacular of all is the Southern Scenic Route. This road takes you along the wild southern coast to the island's southernmost tip, then up to Fiordland and the world-famous Milford Sound.

Car rental is available at all the major airports and can be booked on the Internet, with special deals available. Many people rent motor homes or campers and this makes some of the more inaccessible places available to intrepid travelers.

You can legally drive in New Zealand for up to twelve months if you have either a current driver's license from your home country, or an International Driving Permit (IDP). All drivers, including overseas visitors, must carry their license or permit when driving. You will only be able to drive the same types of vehicles you are licensed to drive in your home country. The common legal age to rent a car in New Zealand is twenty-five years. If your license is not in English, you should be able to provide an official translation. As a visiting driver you should make yourself familiar with New Zealand's traffic laws and safe driving practices which can be found at www. nzta.govt.nz. In New Zealand, all motorists drive on the left-hand side. This is easy to forget when you are tired or distracted, so take care to remind yourself.

The speed limit on the open road is 100 kilometers per hour (approximately 60 miles per hour) and 50 kilometers per hour in built-up areas. You will also encounter other speed limit signs ranging from 70 and 80 kmph through rural hamlets to 20 kmph in city centers and some car parks. Legally you must also slow to 20 kmph when passing a stationary school bus. Drivers and passengers must wear seat belts at all times.

Don't use any "I'm a visitor and did not know the law/ see the sign" excuses for speeding offenses, as police have no discretion, and vehicles that exceed the speed limit by more than 10 kmph are automatically ticketed. Fixed and mobile cameras (often in police cars) are used widely.

Driving under the influence of alcohol or drugs is a serious offense. The rules are strictly enforced, and police carry out breath-test blitzes on expressways and elsewhere, using blood tests where necessary. Most Kiwis are relatively law-abiding and do not run the risk of drinking and driving. They will either use taxis or agree on a sober driver for the evening.

Cycling

New Zealand is rich in stunning scenery and cycling around the country is a rewarding way to appreciate the country. It is a cheap form of travel favored by many, both because it is clean and green, and because of the clear, uncrowded roads.

While some cyclists stick to paved roads, others love the history and varied terrain of the New Zealand Cycle Trail, made up of twenty two Great Rides and twenty five Heartland Rides. Each ride is different. Some are purpose-built tracks where you won't see a car on the whole trail, while others include sections where the road is shared at sections, before veering off into the countryside again.

Renting a bike is easy, and there are plenty of providers in the main centers around each of the trails. Visit www.nzcycletrail.com for a comprehensive list of rides.

Remember that wearing a helmet is mandatory, as it is for motorcyclists. If you're cycling on the road, you must know New Zealand's road rules. *The Official New*

Cycling by Lake Pukaki near Mount Cook, South Island.

Zealand Code for Cyclists, developed by the New Zealand Transport Agency, is a user-friendly guide to New Zealand's traffic laws and safe driving practices.

ACCESSIBILITY

In New Zealand, by law, every new building and major reconstruction must provide "reasonable and adequate" access for people with disabilities.

Every public building must also have accessible bathroom facilities, including those suitable for visitors with limited mobility. Tour operators such as Ability Adventures and Accessible Kiwi Tours provide advice to travelers and holiday packages for individuals and groups. When you're getting around town, most urban transport buses are equipped to cater to wheelchairs and guide dogs.

Two companies that specialize in vehicles for people with disabilities are Freedom Mobility and Disability Car Rentals. Both have wheelchair vehicles and vehicles with hand controls. It is recommended to book ahead.

Parking concessions are available for people with disabilities, and temporary display cards can be issued for the length of a visitor's stay. Disability parking permits issued in other countries do not automatically work in New Zealand. To get a New Zealand mobility parking permit you will need to show your home mobility card or a medical certificate.

WHERE TO STAY

There are plenty of accommodation options, large and small, throughout Aotearoa.

Self-catering motels are a popular choice and you can also find B&Bs and hotels on sites like TripAdvisor and www.aatravel.co.nz. Another option involves staying on a farm. See www.truenz.co.nz/farmstays for ideas.

Many people offer rooms, apartments, and houses on Airbnb and NZ Holiday Homes.

If you're backpacking, there are lodges and hostels everywhere. Sometimes you'll stay at magnificent sites, other times the buildings are older or rundown. Listings can be found at www.bbh.co.nz and www.yha.org.nz.

There are many commercial camping grounds too, and the Department of Conservation has camping sites in all the national parks. There are huts on the tramping trails, which need to be booked in advance. Some are inexpensive, but those on the managed trails cost more. You will probably have to share the hut with other trampers. Kiwis believe that fabulous views and desirable destinations are for everyone to enjoy, so camping and caravan parks are often in prime areas.

HEALTH AND SAFETY

New Zealand has a relatively low crime rate and is generally a very safe place to travel in. However, crime does exist, and you should take the same care with safety and possessions as you would anywhere. Make copies of essential documents like passports and credit cards and keep them separate from the originals. Keep a record of the description and the serial numbers of cameras, tablets, and smartphones, too.

As far as wildlife goes, Aotearoa is very benign. There are no dangerous animals, and the most poisonous invertebrate is the endangered Katipo spider, whose bite can be painful and lead to heart palpitations. Shark attacks are rare, and the many species in waters off the coast probably have more to fear from humans.

Beware the Sun
The hole in the ozone layer is another matter entirely. Ozone is a gas that occurs in the earth's upper atmosphere. Usually, the ozone layer wraps the planet like a blanket, keeping out most of the sun's harmful UV

rays. When humans all over the world discharge ozone-depleting chemicals and pollution into the atmosphere, the ozone layer thins over New Zealand and Australia. Some years are worse than others. The hole in 2020 was the twelfth largest since records began, whereas in 2019, it was one of the smallest.

All this means that the summer sunlight in New Zealand is harsher and more damaging to the skin than the summer sun in the northern hemisphere and levels can be extreme, even when the sky is cloudy. It's essential to use plenty of sunblock with a high UV factor when you go outside. As a rule, try and stay out of direct sunlight between 11:00 a.m. and 4:00 p.m. When you do go out, wear a sunhat and sunglasses to protect your head, neck, and eyes. It's a good idea to cover your shoulders and back, too.

Radio and TV weather forecasters usually include a "burn factor" in their report, which is the amount of time one can stay in the sun without incurring sunburn. Kiwis have been flippant in heeding the "slip, slop, slap, and wrap" message in past years, so there is a lot of skin cancer around. Melanoma killed 363 Kiwis in 2016 alone.

Accidents and Health Care

Anyone who has an accident in New Zealand, including tourists and visitors, has their medical care covered by the Accident Compensation Corporation (ACC). When you visit a doctor or hospital for an injury, you will be asked to fill out a form so that ACC can subsidize your treatment. Still, there are often additional charges to pay.

It's a different matter if you are ill and need a doctor or dentist. Then you'll be asked to pay for the full costs of treatment, which can be awfully expensive. In Queenstown, for example, the overseas visitor's consultation charge in 2021 was $180 (approximately US $130). In contrast, residents who are enrolled with the clinic pay $60.

Hospitals also charge overseas visitors for medical treatment, and even an ambulance ride costs a lot. New Zealand has reciprocal health agreements with the UK and Australia, so their citizens may be covered for hospital care. Overall, it's wise to have comprehensive travel insurance when traveling in New Zealand.

Cancer, including smoking-related cancer, has been the leading cause of death for over ten years, followed by heart disease, while diabetes is also significant. To help combat this, New Zealand has an ambitious "smoke free by 2025" plan. Vaping is on the rise, but cigarette smoking rates are dropping. In 2020, just 12 percent of New Zealanders over the age of fifteen smoked, with fewer young people starting the habit. The Maori adult percentage was higher, at 28.7 percent, but that was still a significant drop from previous decades. Since 2018, all cigarettes have been in plain or standardized packages. They show disturbing pictures of tobacco-inflicted damage and health warnings in English and Maori. Tobacco is heavily taxed too, and if you want to buy a cigarette packet in New Zealand, expect to pay at least $42 (around US $30).

STAYING SAFE OUTDOORS

Most visitors come to New Zealand to enjoy the outstanding natural environment but there are precautions that should be taken. Firstly, take the time to learn about where you are going and to seek advice from your local i-SITE or Department of Conservation (DOC) Visitor Centre on how to be best prepared.

Cell phone: Coverage is unreliable outside the main city centers and if you are venturing into the bush or the mountains you are unlikely to get reception. Consider carrying a personal locator beacon and a battery-powered radio if you are planning any extended hiking stints, especially if you're traveling alone.

Weather: It can be variable and severe at times. Always be prepared for wet, cold weather and on days when it is sunny, remember that New Zealand's clear, unpolluted atmosphere and relatively low latitudes means the sunlight is stronger than in much of Europe or North America. Check weather conditions and any alerts issued by the DOC before you set out. Weather warnings should be treated seriously.

Challenging terrain: Don't underestimate any "walk" outside the main centers. You need to be reasonably fit. Check out the recommended level of fitness required for any walk before you set off. You also need the right clothing and proper footwear.

Tell someone where you are going: Tell someone your plans and leave a date for when to raise the alarm if you haven't returned. Leave a detailed trip plan with the DOC or a friend, including a "panic" date. The more details there are about your intentions, the quicker you'll be rescued if something goes wrong. You'll find a Outdoor Intentions form on www.adventuresmart.org.nz where you can list your route.

Crime

On the whole, New Zealand is a safe and secure country to visit. Although crime is increasing, it has a long way to catch up with the rest of the world. In rural towns, children still leave their bicycles in a hedge for the day before catching the school bus and picking them up in the afternoon. At home, keys are left under the mat for visitors, or the back door is left unlocked. Vegetables, fruit, eggs, and honey are often put out next to an honesty box for payment. None of this happens in the cities, however, where you must always lock houses and cars. Theft is the most frequent crime, particularly stealing from vehicles. Don't leave items on display and hide valuables in the trunk. Take standard safety precautions with your possessions and keep documents such as passports locked up in hotel rooms or a secure place.

Be as cautious as you would be in any city. Don't walk down dark alleys or through parks late at night and keep together in a group if possible.

Be careful when you're out in the wild or hitchhiking. There have been a few highly publicized assaults and murders of overseas trampers over the years, and hitchhiking, though common, always carries a bit of risk.

CHAPTER EIGHT

BUSINESS BRIEFING

New Zealand has a relatively deregulated, open economy and is recognized globally as a safe place to invest. A nation with plenty of economic freedom and one of the least corrupt, in 2020, it ranked first of 190 countries for ease of doing business. New Zealand has a straightforward, business-friendly taxation system that supports capital development, research and development, and international investment. There are sixteen free trade agreements in place, with more in the pipeline, and many container ships regularly enter the six largest ports. Cruise ships sail into New Zealand's beautiful harbors, while global airlines fly visitors and goods into and out of Auckland and Christchurch international airports. (Both cruising and international travel halted during 2020–2021.)

The government rarely provides incentives for people to invest in New Zealand. Instead, it believes that its stable political system and consistent economy will attract overseas investors. Foreign investors must apply for approval before investing in housing, buying land, or fishing assets.

THE KIWI WORKPLACE

Environment
As in other areas of Kiwi life, New Zealand's work environment is often informal and laid-back. Many Kiwis have a good work-life balance, working eight hours a day, with weekends off. Others, who may earn little more than the minimum wage, will work many hours to make ends meet. Small business owners, farmers, and those who are self-employed often work seven days a week. Most New Zealanders are friendly, accommodating, and courteous and expect a similar attitude from you. Rude or demanding behavior at any level will only get you a blank stare.

Management style is often relatively informal, and, in many workplaces, people are often on a first-name basis with their superiors, especially in small to medium enterprises. Staff in these businesses are respectful of managers, but also regard them as one of the team, rather than an unapproachable figurehead.

The Workforce
Aotearoa is a nation of small and micro businesses, including an increasing number who are self-employed or entrepreneurs. According to the

Ministry for Business, Innovation, and Employment, there are around 530,000 small businesses (defined as those with fewer than 20 employees). These make up 97 percent of all New Zealand firms and account for more than one-quarter of the GDP.

Approximately two-thirds of adults are full-time workers, and others have part-time jobs. Over 50 percent have some flexibility in their work hours, and nowadays, many can work from home for at least part of the week.

The public sector employs 5 percent of the total workforce in New Zealand. That figure jumps to 18 percent when you include education, health, and local government. However, the majority of New Zealanders work in service industries. These include community, social and personal services, wholesale and retail trade, restaurants, and hotels. In 2021, nearly 20 percent of the workforce was in manufacturing and industry, with a further 5 percent working in agriculture. Unemployment was around 4.9 percent at the end of 2020. However, some commentators argue that the actual number is higher, as many potential workers are on sickness or job-seeker benefits.

Workers Unions were influential in the twentieth century. In fact, New Zealand was once one of the most unionized countries in the world. However, union membership has dwindled in recent years, with most employees being encouraged to have individual contracts, though it is illegal for an employer not to allow someone to join a union if they wish to. In 2021, approximately only 10 percent of workers belonged to a union, down from 16 percent in 2013.

Women in the Workplace

New Zealand strives to be an egalitarian society, and the Equal Pay Act of 1972 made different pay rates between men and women illegal. However, because women still tend to be more heavily employed in lower-paid industries, overall, men tend to have higher salaries. In 2020 just over 30 percent of directors in listed companies were women, and New

Prime Minister Jacinda Ardern became the world's youngest female head of state at age thirty-seven.

Zealand is still well behind many other countries in appointing female CEOs and senior managers. Women are being actively encouraged to seek business leadership positions, however, and in the public sector, the numbers of women and men in management roles are about equal.

MAKING APPOINTMENTS

Personal connections can be important for visiting businesspeople, but if you don't have a personal contact make an appointment anyway. It's easier to find the right person if you explain what you need and that you're unsure who to talk to. Also, be aware that key personnel may be away during prime vacation times and that many companies close completely over Christmas and the first two weeks of January, especially lawyers, accountants, district councils, and finance firms.

MEETINGS

Many New Zealand businesses have a "dress-for-your-day" approach, which means that less formal attire is appropriate in the office, while more formal clothes, namely a suit, is expected at important meetings. Women wear suits, trousers, skirts or dresses, and shirts or tops.

Meetings are often relaxed and friendly and may include lunch. Many smaller meetings take place in restaurants or cafés over coffee. Make sure you're on time for meetings because lateness can give the impression that you're unreliable.

You will probably be on first-name terms from the start and it's acceptable to stand or sit in a relaxed manner. However, don't misinterpret this lack of formality; this is still a business conversation. It's best to show professionalism, integrity, and a straightforward approach.

You can expect a certain amount of small talk before getting down to business. You'll find it helpful to know about the latest happenings in New Zealand, especially some of the week's latest sporting fixtures. There are likely to be comments on the weather, too, especially if it is unusual for the current season.

PRESENTATIONS

If you're giving a presentation, stick to facts and don't exaggerate. Kiwis would rather have down-to-earth, honest observations and comments than vague promises or hyped sales talk.

People will expect to see some history of your product or service, as well as testimonials, and references. Preferably, show your knowledge and understanding of relevant local conditions, too.

Do your homework on customs requirements, government regulations, and industrial relations before you come. The New Zealand Embassy, Consulate, or Trade Attaché in your country can supply the correct information and clarify what is expected and appropriate.

Respect people's personal space but maintain some eye contact around the room. It's appropriate to include some relevant humor, especially as an icebreaker in your opening remarks. However, don't use a lot of slang, and avoid profanity, as that will lose respect in a business context.

NEGOTIATING

Kiwis should not be hurried during the negotiating or decision-making process. They will not appreciate numerous follow-up calls, high-pressure sales tactics, close deadlines, or the like. Be aware, too, that they are not always diligent about returning calls. You should demonstrate a product's capability rather than talk about it. Don't over-sell your product, but don't skimp on explaining terms and conditions either. Be sure you have included everything relevant.

Be realistic with costs. New Zealanders will haggle a little over prices but like to end up with value for money and a fair deal for everyone. Be concise, straightforward, honest, and direct. It is also vital that you stick to your undertakings; don't make promises you can't keep. Kiwis are very trusting until they are given a reason not to be, and it is difficult to heal a broken business relationship. If you muck them around or break your promises, they won't continue working with you. However, if you build up a good business relationship, it will be worthwhile, as New Zealanders are loyal and fair.

CONTRACTS

Shake hands on a deal but get it down on paper to ensure there are no misunderstandings. Your contract should cover all the details and leave no room for doubt. Kiwi firms can be both pedantic about tiny discrepancies and oblivious to major howlers, so be prepared for all contingencies and double-check the details.

RESOLVING DISPUTES

New Zealand is not a litigious society. You would have to be very unfortunate if a dispute arose and legal recourse was the only option. Kiwis, by and large, do not like confrontation and would make a considerable effort to avoid this. However, if there is disagreement, then tackle it—don't beat around the bush—and look at the options. Try to get everyone's commitment to solving the problem before looking at possible ways of doing so. Mediation with a good facilitator is preferable to legal action because it is less costly in money, time, and stress.

LEGISLATION

New Zealand has a great deal of legislation concerning employment. All employees are entitled to a minimum wage, annual leave, and public holidays. There are also entitlements to sick and bereavement leave, arrangements for those working on public holidays, and directions as to calculating holiday pay. All employees are entitled to a minimum of four weeks' annual leave as well as the eleven paid public holidays.

Parental leave is available to both partners around the birth of a child, and to those adopting a child under the age of five. Employees must have worked for at least twelve months, with an average of ten hours a week prior to the anticipated date of birth. In 2020 paid maternity leave was increased from eighteen to twenty-six weeks. It is usually taken by mothers but can be used by either parent. Fathers can also take two weeks of paternity leave after the birth. There is also the option to take a further twenty-six weeks unpaid leave, allowing for a year of maternity leave altogether.

WORKING IN NEW ZEALAND

To work in New Zealand, you need to be a citizen or permanent resident or have a work permit or appropriate visa. You must apply for all work visas in advance and many, though not all, require you to be in possession of a job offer in order to qualify. One short-term option is the New Zealand Working Holiday Scheme (WHS) which allows you to be in New Zealand for up to twelve months and to work for up to three months for any one employer. WHS visas are extended to twenty-three months for British and Canadian citizens. See www.immigration.govt.nz for more on which visas are available.

New Zealand has a straightforward tax system for employees. It's called PAYE—Pay As You Earn—and it means that an employer will deduct taxes from your wages before you receive your pay. You'll need an IRD number and to know the correct tax code to ensure that the right amount of tax is deducted; otherwise, you can find yourself paying too much.

If you are a tax resident in your home country, they may tax your worldwide incomes, including income earned in New Zealand. Some countries have double taxation agreements with New Zealand to avoid that happening. To know where you stand, go to www.ird.govt.nz.

Qualifying for citizenship includes being a permanent resident intending to stay in the country. You also need to be of good character, speak some

English, and understand New Zealand citizenship's responsibilities and privileges. Citizenship ceremonies are held by local councils and include speeches, cultural performances, and the national anthem. The new citizens take an oath or affirmation of allegiance and then receive their citizenship certificate. Afterwards, new citizens may apply for a New Zealand passport if they wish.

BECOMING A KIWI

The laws governing naturalization have changed considerably over the years. Up to 1986, immigration policy focused on nationality and ethnic origin for

acceptance. Since then, the emphasis has been on specific educational, professional, business, age, and skills requirements, regardless of nationality or race. Immigrants are selected according to the three main categories: skills and business, family ties, and humanitarian reasons.

The system is designed to attract those immigrants most needed in the country, which also serves to control numbers. Minimum standards of English are now required. For the skilled migrant category and specific business categories, the level is the equivalent of university admittance. Today's process is centered on a points system. Points are awarded according to age, qualifications, work experience, employment status, the skills shortage in the country, and the specific job offer. Applicants also have to be of good health and character. All medical and X-ray certificates must be less than three months old when an application is filed.

The New Zealand Immigration Service now also applies much stricter rules, making it harder to get into the country if you have a troublesome medical history. (Current policy says that an applicant should not be a potential burden on the health service.)

There is more encouragement for migrants to enter via the skilled/business category. Skilled workers include health professionals (nurses, doctors, and technicians), seasonal agricultural workers, engineering, construction, trades, and ITC professionals. There are also entrepreneur visas and an investor category for those who intend to contribute a minimum of NZ $1 million. Investor Plus applicants need at least NZ $10 million to invest. Entrepreneurs need to prove the establishment of a successful business in New Zealand. Employees of relocating companies and those planning to establish a business may also be eligible.

The family-sponsored stream contributes around 30 percent of total immigration numbers, usually partners and dependent children, and the international humanitarian stream makes up the remaining 10 percent. It includes refugees and Pacific Islanders who are given special access.

In 2018, the top five source countries for migrants were China, India, UK, South Africa, and the Philippines.

CHAPTER NINE

COMMUNICATING

LANGUAGE

New Zealand has three official languages: English, Te Reo Maori, and New Zealand Sign Language. The most widely of these is English and it's spoken with a distinct accent which evolved from the melting pot of English, Irish, Scottish, Welsh, and Australian migrants who joined the Maori in New Zealand's early days.

The most noticeable characteristic of the Kiwi accent is the way that vowel sounds are flattened, especially "a," "e," and "i" which can cause some confusion. For example, you'll hear New Zealanders saying "fush and chups" when they mean fish and chips, "ket" instead of cat, and "pits" when they're talking about their pets.

Many New Zealanders barely pronounce the letter "r" in some words, so that "farm" can sound more like "fahm." In Southland, however, the opposite is true, and there you'll hear the word as "farrrm." Kiwis from

181

further north can always tell a Southlander by the way they roll their Rs.

Many Kiwis also talk quickly which can make it hard to catch what they're saying at first, a problem compounded by the fact that many don't move their lips much or open their mouths very wide. On the other hand, Maori and Pasifika people have a slower and more lyrical way of speaking.

Visitors will notice that Kiwis often have a rising inflection at the end of their sentences, making it seem as if they're asking a question. Maori in particular often end their sentences with "eh" (pronounced ay); it's not a word, more an emphatic sound that can mean anything from "do you agree with me?" to "do you understand what I'm saying?"

Learning the Lingo

There's a certain amount of vocabulary that is unique to New Zild, the name by which locals affectionally refer to their particular brand of English. For example, in Chapter 5 we discussed the holiday homes called "bachs" and in Chapter 6, how "bring a plate" means contributing food at a party. Well, there's plenty more.

If everything's going well, a Kiwi might tell you it's "sweet as," or "a box of birds." In summer, they put food for the "barbie" (barbecue) into a "chilly bin" (portable cooler). They wear "togs" (swimming costumes) at the beach and "jandals" (flip-flop sandals) on their feet. And if someone says, "it's my shout," they mean they will pay for the drinks or food.

The word "bugger" is not considered offensive in New Zealand; sometimes it's used to refer to a person (as in, "he's a good bugger,") or to an unfavorable event. For example, in Christchurch, after the 2011 earthquake, "it was a real bugger" that everything was "munted" (broken).

If you plan to stay in the country for a while, and maybe consider renting or even buying a home, then a whole new vocabulary is necessary. For instance, if you prefer the countryside to live in, refer to it as the "wopwops," or even "backblocks," which is a term originally given to land bought from Maori but that came to mean "more remote farming." A piece of land is called a "block." Asking for a "plot" will result in your being shown the nearest cemetery! If requiring something a little bigger than a "block," then "section" or "lifestyle block" are the terms.

When you ask Kiwis a question, they'll often start their reply with "yeah, nah." Confusingly, that could mean yes or no; it's really just an extra sound (like um) to give yourself time to think. Things are often "awesome" in New Zealand, but, confusingly, they could also be described as "mean" which is most often used as a word of praise.

"Chur" is a flexible North Island expression meaning thanks or cheers. New Zealanders are fond of abbreviations and will often tack an "ie" or "o" onto the end of words. So, for example, presents become "prezzies," cousins become "cuzzies," and—in rural New Zealand—the morning tea is called a "smoko."

In America or England, you might go hiking in a forest with a stream running through it. But in New Zealand, you'll be "tramping in the bush," and your stream will become a "creek." These are just a few of the hundreds of words and expressions that might have you wondering what your Kiwi mate meant. Don't worry—if you don't understand, just ask. New Zealanders are used to visitors who are puzzled by the lingo.

Te Reo Maori

In the early 1900s, there was a conscious effort to suppress the Maori language, known as Te Reo Maori, and children were punished for speaking it at school. As a result, several generations of Maori grew up not speaking Te Reo, and the language was in danger of completely dying out. Since the 1970s, however, there has been a concerted effort to revive and revitalize the language, emphasizing Maori cultural practices and including up-to-date vocabulary. Nowadays, approximately 50,000 people speak Te Reo fluently, and many more are learning. There are also moves afoot to make learning Te Reo compulsory in schools, though many schools already incorporate the language into classrooms where possible. Many places in Aotearoa are known by their Maori names, while others have dual names in Te Reo and English, and both are used in conversation and on written signs.

The National Anthem, God Defend New Zealand, also has a Maori and an NZ Sign Language version. Usually, the first verse is sung in Te Reo, then repeated

SOME COMMON TE REO MAORI WORDS

Kia-ora hello or thank you

Tēnā koe hello, thank you (to one person)

Tēnā koutou hello to more than two people

Nau Mai, haere mai welcome

Whanau family

Mahi work

Motu island, country

Hui meeting

Hikoi long walk (often a protest march)

Iwi tribe

Kai food

Puku belly

Ka kite ano (goodbye, see you again)

Haere a goodbye

Tangata whenua people of the land, local people

in English. Nowadays, Kiwis never use the remaining verses of their anthem. Probably, many don't even know there are other verses, but it's worth looking them up, as there are some beautiful sentiments which express the Kiwi way of looking at the world. New Zealand's second national anthem is "God Save The Queen." It is rarely used, and mainly reserved for the rare occasions when British royalty visits the country.

Te Reo Maori is evident in more than just spoken, colloquial language. It is becoming part of the language of NZ officialdom. Many terms are now commonly used in the media and legislation without an accompanying English translation. It is now so usual, that the television complaints authority announced in 2021 that it would no longer receive or acknowledge any complaints about the use of Te Reo in television and radio programs.

COMMUNICATION STYLES

As we have seen, New Zealanders are generally unpretentious, informal, and down to earth, and prefer it if you adopt a similar approach. You are not expected to prove yourself in any way and will be taken at face value, at least to start with. However, too much directness can be taken for aggression, and too much familiarity is not appreciated, at least initially. As such, it is wise to tread carefully until you are better acquainted. For example, don't ask a lot of personal questions; if you do, Kiwis will quickly retreat. However, they would be more than happy to answer more general questions about the country, the way of life, and other related topics.

Kiwis are not backslapping types and it is important to respect their personal space; an arm's length is generally enough. A handshake is the most common greeting, although friends will often exchange hugs when one or both are women. Kiwi men are less likely to hug each other when they meet, but you'll see male sports players and other stars hugging after a big victory or hard-fought loss.

Some common greetings include "How are ya?" (often rolled into one word), and "How's it going?" These are equivalent to greetings like "Good morning!" rather than actual inquiries after your health. The usual response is a simple, "Good, thanks." You might also notice Kiwis catching your eye and then raising their eyebrows, or nodding and smiling, both of which are informal acknowledgments of your presence.

Kiwis are happy to receive compliments about their homes, decor, possessions, and so on, especially as icebreakers. They are not so good at accepting compliments about themselves. That is possibly because Kiwis are expected to be modest about their accomplishments. Don't let that stop you from offering genuine praise, though. They might make self-deprecating comments, but deep down they'll enjoy the affirmation.

"No-nos"

Swearing, or cursing, has become part of everyday language among some New Zealanders, while others prefer to keep coarser language out of their vocabulary. As such, it's probably best to err on the side of caution until you know who you're talking to. The "f—" word is frowned on in business or formal situations, though you may hear it used in casual conversation.

The legal drinking age is eighteen, and there are stiff penalties for selling alcohol to someone underage. While you do see it happening, especially late on a Friday or Saturday night, getting drunk in public is generally considered offensive. There is also concern about the increase in teenagers drinking alcohol, despite the penalties involved.

In New Zealand, the alcohol limit for drivers aged twenty years and over is 250 micrograms (mcg) of alcohol per liter of breath, and the blood alcohol limit is 50 milligrams (mg) per 100 milliliters (ml) of blood. If you are under twenty, the alcohol limit for drivers is zero. Most drivers are careful to keep under this limit because the penalties include losing their driver's license and hefty fines. Repeat offenders are likely to find themselves in jail.

Be careful about gestures, as what means something in one society is often not the same in another. Former US president George Bush's flashing of the "V for victory" sign to Australians in 1992 being a good example—in Australia and New Zealand, that's the equivalent of putting up a middle finger in the US.

Don't forget that, for the Maori, the *marae* (meeting ground) is considered sacrosanct (see page 74). Be aware also that some Maori and Samoans may avoid prolonged eye contact out of a sense of respect. Similarly, ensure that you do not sit higher than a Polynesian counterpart, which is considered rude.

HUMOR

Kiwis have a dry sense of humor, which is frequently used to put themselves and others at ease. They particularly enjoy tongue-in-cheek quips and are most fond of jokes that are either self-deprecating—or those that poke fun at Aussies! Most Kiwis like to tease, but it is usually good-natured and is not meant to be taken literally, or to give offense.

Kiwi humor can also be somewhat dark or gruesome, especially when being used to make a point. Air New Zealand is well known for its humorous safety videos and a recent anti-drink-driving campaign portrayed a teen victim of a drunken accident haunting his mates and offering them "ghost chips."

Other times it borders on the absurd, "taking the mickey" out of everyday situations. Household names include Flight of the Conchords, Rhys Darby, and Rose Matafeo. Local talent can be found performing in bars around Auckland and at the city's annual International Comedy Festival.

MAIL SERVICES

New Zealand's national postal service, NZ Post, is efficient and reliable. Mail is delivered to houses and private mailboxes three times a week, and the postage cost is based on the size and weight of your letter or document. E-mail has had a devastating effect on the profitability of NZ Post. As fewer letters are being sent, many post shops have closed, or been incorporated into bookshops. Where they do exist, they are open every day except Saturday afternoons and Sundays.

Parcel delivery, on the other hand, is increasing year on year as New Zealanders embrace online shopping. You can send parcels through NZ Post or its courier business, CourierPost. Other courier companies also offer same-day or overnight delivery services throughout the country. All companies run track and trace services which allow customers to check on an item at any time from pick-up to delivery.

There are several overseas mail services. International Express is the NZ Post track and trace courier service and delivers to more than 220 countries within days, and Australia the next morning. International Air delivers in three to ten days, with track and trace facilities to some countries.

A Poste Restante, or mail holding service, is available at some post offices, which will store letters and parcels less than 30 kg for up to two months. The service is free of charge for the first seven days, then charges mount the longer an item is held.

INTERNET

New Zealanders have embraced the Internet as a way of keeping connected and doing business. By January 2021, Internet penetration in New Zealand, i.e. the percentage of the total population that uses the Internet, was at

94 percent which compares favorably to 90 percent in the US and 94.6 percent in the UK.

Most homes and businesses connect to the Internet via copper wire or fiberoptic cable. Broadband connections aren't possible in some rural or isolated properties which instead use modems that connect to the Internet via cell phone towers or satellites. These connections are fast but more expensive than city connections, which are often bundled with electricity and gas services.

Like many others around the world, New Zealanders learned to work from home in 2020 because of the pandemic. Shopping online and click and collect services increased markedly during that year and continue to be popular because of their ease and convenience.

According to DataReportal, the number of social media users in New Zealand in 2021 was equivalent to 82 percent of the population. Facebook and Instagram were the most popular platforms for Kiwis, followed by Pinterest and Twitter.

SIM CARDS AND CELL PHONES

Most New Zealanders own at least one cell phone, or mobile phone, as they are known locally. The majority of these are smartphones. The leading mobile phone providers are Spark, Vodafone, and 2degrees. Together, these companies have a 90 percent share in New Zealand's telecoms market.

Don't try to use International Roaming in New Zealand. It's costly, and people often won't return your calls if they see that you're using an overseas number. Spark, Vodafone, 2degrees, and Skinny all have suitable plans for visitors, and it will be cheaper and more convenient for you to buy a SIM card from one of these providers. Mobile plans are either prepaid or monthly plans, which include phone calls, SMS texting, and varying amounts of mobile Internet data. Free Wi-Fi hotspots are found in main cities and transport hubs, but are harder to locate in rural areas.

Most of the places you'll go to in New Zealand will have mobile phone coverage. Blind spots include national parks, mountain passes, and smaller islands. 4G is the most common network, with 5G available in some cities as of 2021, with more locations to follow.

Many Kiwis use messaging apps to communicate. Facebook Messenger is the most popular, followed by WhatsApp, Snapchat, Skype, and Facetime. The Houseparty app for group video chat became popular during the pandemic, while others discovered Viber and Discord. Banking apps are also on the rise, making it easy to bank online or through your smartphone.

When mobiles first appeared in New Zealand, phone calls were comparatively expensive, and SMS or "texting" was cheap, and, as a result, New Zealanders were great texters in those days. Now, most mobile plans make it as cost-effective to phone people within New Zealand as it is to text.

Because mobiles are so popular, there are fewer public phone boxes in New Zealand than in the past. However, you can usually find one in places such as airports and shopping centers. You can buy cards for these phone boxes as well as mobile prepay top-ups at supermarkets, bookshops, and service stations.

Most businesses still use landline telephones, but at least one in five Kiwi homes no longer has a landline, relying on their mobiles instead. One reason for this is cost; landline calls are free within your local area, but calls to other regions are expensive compared to calling on your mobile or a messaging app. In addition there is a monthly line-rental fee even if you don't make any calls. New Zealand landline phone numbers can be found online in the White Pages (including business and residential), the Yellow Pages (business category listings), and in printed phone books that are delivered to homes and businesses.

USEFUL TELEPHONE NUMBERS

111 Emergency number for all services. An operator will direct you to the Police, Fire, or Ambulance service.

*555 Mobile telephone number to report non-emergency traffic incidents such as a breakdown, car crash with no injuries, or road hazards

018 National Directory Assistance

0172 International Directory Inquiries

CONCLUSION

New Zealand is a long way from the rest of the world—but it is well worth the journey. It is a country of beauty, charm, and great diversity. Most tourists find it exciting and adventurous, but also a relaxing, peaceful place to visit. The time zone usually means that people are rising just when much of the world is going to sleep, and vice versa. That means you can regale your family with the day's adventures while they're sipping their morning coffee. Kiwis are well used to this and to being far from anywhere and anything. Being an isolated island nation does have its advantages—the coronavirus pandemic being a case in point.

As we've seen, there's a lot to see and do at all times of the year. The wine is internationally renowned, the beer is plentiful, and the food is so varied that boredom is never an option.

The people of New Zealand are informal, nonjudgmental, friendly, and kind. From the local "postie" (mail carrier) to the man behind the counter in the dairy, to the average Kiwi on the street, you will find a readiness to stop, help, and direct you if you're lost. Sometimes, you won't even have to ask—looking uncertainly at a map practically guarantees that someone will offer assistance. Similarly, because most Kiwis are trusting and honest, you can often ask them to watch your luggage while you nip to the bathroom at the airport; you can even leave a key under a flowerpot for plumbers or electricians to let themselves into your house. That sense of well-being and ease is a rarity in much of the Western world today, and something Kiwis have learned not to take for granted.

FURTHER READING

Atkinson, Brett et al. *New Zealand*. Lonely Planet, 2021.

Catton, Eleanor. *The Luminaries*. Victoria: Victoria University Press, 2013. (Won the 2013 Man Booker Prize; adapted into a BBC/TVNZ television miniseries in 2020.)

Grace, Patricia. *Cousins*. Auckland: Penguin, republished 2021. (Movie adaptation, 2021.)

Hulme, Keri. *The Bone People*. USA: Penguin non-classics, 1986. (Won the Booker Prize in 1985.)

Ihimaera, Witi. *Navigating the Stars; Maori Creation Myths*. Auckland: Penguin, 2020.

Ihimaera, Witi. *The Whale Rider*. Auckland: Reed Publishing, 1987, republished 2008. (Movie adaptation, 2002.)

King, Michael. *Penguin History of New Zealand*. Auckland: Penguin,republished 2012. (Widely considered the best and most readable history of New Zealand. Won Readers Choice award in 2004.)

Mansfield, Katherine. *The Garden Party and Other Stories*. Penguin Classics, republished 2008. (The iconic NZ short story writer's most well-known collection.)

Tunney, Susan. *Do They Speak English Down There?* CreateSpace Independent Publishing Platform, 2016.

Walker, Tangaroa. *Farm for Life; Mahi, Mana and Life on the Land*. Auckland: Penguin, 2021.

USEFUL APPS

Travel and Transportation

Air New Zealand App Useful for flight bookings, checking in, and more with NZ's national airline.

CamperMate Provides info on the best campsites, hotels, and hostels nearby as well as amenities like petrol stations. Features reviews and images from other users. Covers both NZ and Australia.

Electric Scooters available in numerous cities by **Flamingo, Beam, Neuron, Lime**, and **Jump**.

Great Rides For the best downloadable cycling trails and amenities.

Google Maps Probably the best map app for NZ coverage.

Uber, Ola, and **Zoomy** For cabs in Auckland, Wellington, and Christchurch. Uber also operates in Dunedin, Hamilton, and Tauranga.

Food and Shopping

Door Dash NZ's most popular food delivery app. Alternatives include **Menulog**, **UberEats**, and **Deliveroo**.

TradeMe NZ's version of eBay and Craigslist combined. (App only available on the NZ app store.)

Activities and NZ Info

BookMe; Grab One; Treat Me; Groupon Discount sites for goods, activities, and food.

Met Service Reliable weather forecasting in NZ.

NZ Covid Tracer App Scan QR codes for contract tracing in the event of an outbreak.

100% Pure New Zealand Destinations, travel itineraries, accommodation, and more.

PICTURE CREDITS

INDEX

Acknowledgements

Thank you to everyone who generously shared their experiences of living and working in New Zealand with me, and to all those who gave so much time and thought to answering my questions. Thanks are also due to my husband, family, and friends for their unwavering support.